HH (47) GAN6350 / £2.50



Published in 2021 by

Russell House Publishing Ltd
The Coach House
Ware
Lyme Regis
Dorset
DT7 3RH
UK

Tel: (+44) 01297 443948

E-mail: jan@russellhouse.co.uk

Website: www.russellhouse.co.uk



British Library Cataloguing-in-Publication Data.

A catalogue record for this book is available from the British Library.

**ISBN: 978-1-9160276-7-1**

## ABOUT THE AUTHOR

Frankie Hudson began her career as a modern language teacher before setting up and managing the UK's first local authority educational unit for school-age mothers in Bristol.

Her experience of the emotional needs of her pupils led her into sex and relationships education with young people, counselling, and counselling training. She has a private practice as a counsellor and counselling supervisor.

Alongside her counselling work, Frankie is an artist and mosaicist; she enjoys singing and playing the cello. She lives with her husband in Bristol.

Additional Publications:

Frances Hudson and Bernard Ineichen, 1991. **Taking it Lying Down: Sexuality and Teenage Motherhood** – Macmillan Educational. ISBN: 978-0-3335317-8-5.

Frankie Hudson, 2019. **We can work it out, Understanding ourselves and our relationships** – Russell House Publishing Ltd. ISBN: 978-1-9160276-3-3.

## ACKNOWLEDGMENTS

I am totally indebted to all my students and clients of all ages and backgrounds. Over the years their persistent encouragement prompted me finally to turn my quick sketches into a book which would be available to all, and not just to those training or seeking support.

To Dennis Hughes and Nick Stephenson I owe an enormous debt of gratitude for their close professional scrutiny and detailed appraisal of the material, as well as pertinent and sensitive suggestions.

To my publisher Jan Baker, I cannot give enough thanks for her long-suffering and patience as I grappled with the whole process of putting the book together.

To Graham Hyde, my thanks for his uninhibited critique and quiet prodding; and for the relief I felt at his instant and positive response to my request that he design the cover. For extra technical help and advice, my thanks also to Ken Patterson.

I am grateful to Human Givens; their practical contribution to the world of counselling has inspired and influenced me all my working life.

Alongside the whole process has been my husband, David Emmerson. His steadfast support, tolerance, patience, and technical know-how have been vital throughout. Without him I might well have lost heart. I remind him again; you are the harmony to my song.

## TABLE OF CONTENTS

# INTRODUCTION

As a teacher then counsellor for many years, one of my major interests and concerns has always been our quest for clarity and understanding in our relationships; all the while curious and smiling at the way we so easily get things wrong.

Knowing that a sense of humour is vital to our health – mental, emotional, and physical – the metaphor comes into its own; the simplest drawings can provide the most powerful message where words just don't do the job. An image has the power to conjure up memories, suggest plans, give us a boost, even inspire; and if it resonates with us - it draws a smile. And we can relax a little.

Our relationships with others begin with ourselves; strange as it may seem, it's difficult to be meaningfully part of a friendship, a team, a couple, if we're not content with ourselves; or if there's something about our circumstances which disappoints us or causes tension or confrontation in our lives. Starting with self-awareness, this book takes us on a journey towards greater understanding and compassion towards ourselves and others, each in our own situation and set of circumstances. Hints and small challenges provide prompts all the way through for experimenting with new insights and ideas for action, change or just reflecting. The added ingredient which travels with us throughout is our ability to smile at ourselves at some of our – let's say – weaker points. The last section is designed to lead us with encouragement and confidence for our emotional life, and so for our relationships.

To start at the beginning.... From the moment we're born we're dependant on our parents and significant others for how we learn about and form our relationships as we grow up. And it starts with recognising that we all begin with a collection of needs and resources which stay with us throughout our life.

This is explained succinctly by the Human Givens approach to counselling [(i)]. It's important torecognise that 'counselling' is just one of many ways of helping people who are in need of personalised support, however complicated or difficult the issues are that they're encountering. In embarking on this book of metaphors about our relationships I am indebted to this approach as a way of seeing and understanding the human condition and how to strive to live in a healthy and balanced way with ourselves and others. Along with other named approaches for 'helping', the Human Givens have sat with me most comfortably for years, underpinning all my work. Yet it was not on any of my counselling training syllabuses [(ii)].

For me, their concepts make absolute sense and read like a simple, easy-to-understand and common-sense philosophy. The basic idea consists of two main aspects of human nature with which we are born: Needs and Resources. These are the 'Givens'.

Our needs at birth are both physiological and emotional. Needs of course must be met for good physical health as we grow up and develop, as well as for our emotional and mental well-being. Both needs sets require care and attention; the physical needs are evident and visible – food and water, warmth, and shelter, for example - while the emotional needs are more subtle, less easily noticed or understood, yet equally essential. When too many of our physical and emotional needs are not met, or when our resources are used incorrectly – unwittingly or otherwise - we suffer considerable distress. And so do those around us (Human Givens 2013).

The list of emotional needs may itself be an eye-opener. Included in this list are security; trust; autonomy; control; intimacy; connection with others; and to be stretched and appropriately challenged in all that we try. However, depending on our life circumstances and environment, these needs may or may not be fully met. At this time of writing, in these days of the coronavirus pandemic, these aspects of our emotional life are emerging as vitally evident; the fact that many of these needs are blatantly unmeetable during this period only emphasise the truth of this. After all, it's difficult to feel in control and connect with others during lockdown; yet very important to keep our sense of humour. The focus on our emotional needs remains essential; our imaginative and creative attempts at finding ways of managing show the power and the quality of our resources.

We are so driven by our feelings that, without emotional awareness and stability, we feel unfulfilled. As children we accept our life and experiences, we take what's on offer for granted as 'normal'. We may not know anything is missing until much later, and, in consequence, in a fog of confusion, we may well experience misunderstandings and unhappiness in adulthood. Emotional/mental as well as physiological development are equally essential for our potential total good health and general well-being.

Our innate resources of intelligence, memory, imagination, creativity, inspiration, and problem-solving skills – to name but a few – can help us recognise what we need today and go some way to achieving that. Added to this is the potential to strive and achieve as far and as much as we feel the urge. Of course, these resources may well not be in their full use in adulthood. There is always the possibility for further development. I believe whole-heartedly that it is never too late to work at something or try something new.

Another basic concept in the Human Givens is pattern-matching; this can be useful as well as unhelpful, in that our memory will automatically go to a past experience for information as to how to deal with a similar experience in the present, whether it be a happy or unhappy one. If we think about it, what else can we do? We only have our individual experience of the world on which to base our understanding of things today.

The aim of this book is to encourage a balanced view of ourselves and our way of relating. It seems straightforward to see our lives as underpinned by the importance of our needs being met from the very beginning; and, as we develop, being able and encouraged to use our innate resources throughout our lives. Relating to ourselves might seem strange, but we need to know ourselves before we can be relaxed and real with others. Our habits, our life- style, our likes and dislikes, our sense of humour; our moods, enthusiasms, fears and so on are all different parts of what makes us who we are. You will recognise your own with a wry smile. How we relate to others as friends, lovers, parents, siblings, teachers, colleagues, etc., depends enormously on how we feel and understand ourselves.

We do not live in a vacuum. As human beings, we need social connection, closeness, intimacy; and, at the time of writing, today as never before, we're living with the restrictions caused by all that has transpired by society's response to Covid 19. With our 'Givens' we have the capacity to make and maintain relationships of all kinds, and to pass this capacity on to our children; and yet for months and months this need for contact has been very difficult to meet. We are finding that the cost to us of this loss is taking its toll on our well-being, our physical and particularly mental health. This book is to help keep our spirits up.

My experience of working with children and families; couples; young people and adults; as teacher, researcher, counselling trainer and psychotherapist, also as a mother, have given me – and continue to give - a rich sense of the variety of personalities, foibles, habits, difficulties, crises, and heartache that make up the human condition and experience.

The ideas here are expressed in metaphors by line drawings. I was taught this short-cut by my students and clients over the years; it was they who encouraged me to publish the drawings because "they speak to everybody, not just your students/clients". They pointed out that this unthreatening and humorous way of seeing and explaining our behaviour and our relationships was not only useful for them but also pretty essential for anyone who is curious about themselves and their relationships, and open to reflection and change. Without this huge nudge, I would probably not be writing this now. My gratitude extends to you all – you know who you are!

A simple drawing can give a strong message where words often fail to make sense to us. In these pages you may find helpful ideas and suggestions to support your quest for greater self-understanding, for improved relationships and a life balance which offers you meaning and purpose appropriate for you.

Although it was not my intention at the outset, this book may be a self-help book for you. And although it has a journey, a direction of sorts, for you it may be more a book for dipping into, to bring a smile of recognition and understanding here and there. Its purpose is to be useful, interesting, encouraging and motivating.

I hope the idea of the Givens – Needs and Resources, and how they relate to you - will emerge as you explore these pages, where I also hope you will find some amusement.

(i) www.humangivens.com/publications

(ii) **Griffiths J, Tyrrell I**, 2013. **Human Givens: The new approach to emotional health and clear thinking**, H G Publishing, ISBN: 978-1-89939831-7.

# SECTION 1

## UNDERSTANDING OURSELVES

This section is about raising awareness of our habits; getting to know 'how we tick', how we comfort ourselves, what upsets us and our reactions; how we get ourselves heard and how we cope when upset or irritated.

Understanding our strengths and vulnerabilities, our Resources and Needs, goes a long way to help us to feel more confident and hopeful. Recognising and affirming our skills and abilities, while becoming aware of what might be missing, can both encourage and motivate us to look more closely at aspects of ourselves that we would like to change.

Do we sometimes over-do things? Do we say or do things which we later wish we hadn't? And wonder why? You may find some of the metaphors here resonate with you, whether you recognise your own characteristics and behaviours, or those of others.

We first learn to be us by copying and repeating, and by the way those around us – parents, carers and significant others – treat us and behave with each other. Our learning is embedded and rewarded by receiving positive and affirming responses which mean our behaviour is approved of. These early templates stay with us as patterns to match in later life. As we shall learn during the course of this book, we can be caught out by this pattern-matching; depending on the circumstances, this can be to our advantage or disadvantage.

In this section you may become more aware of aspects of your life where, through no fault of your own, some of your innate needs were not met. Hopefully you will be able to reconnect with some of your 'given' resources; and recognise pattern-matching behaviours.

Acknowledging our vulnerability, and needs not met, can be seen as one of our strengths. A paradox? See what you think.

# Learning Cycle!

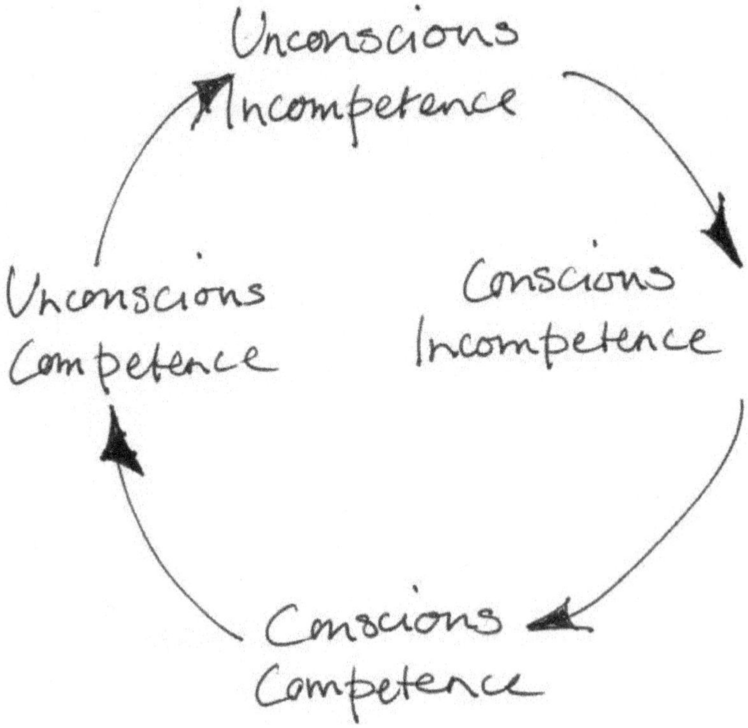


Ref: David Kolb 1974

## Learning cycle 1

One way of understanding how we manage to effect change – change our behaviour or learn a new skill - is to cast our mind back to how we ever learnt anything at school. If we think back to those days and the way we sometimes struggled with getting our heads round sums, the meaning of words, music, poetry, etc., or learning to play an instrument, or reading, understanding and even speaking a foreign language.... It's now obvious that the way to learn anything is by imitation and repetition, whether it's mental or physical effort that's required.

The learning cycle is fluid - for good reason. We can move around on it, re-evaluate where we've got to. 'If at first you don't succeed, try and try again'. And without continuous practice we can too easily slip back. Remember: 'If you don't use it, you lose it'.

Given that we're born with potential for competence, this cycle very simply helps us understand the process of learning new skills as well as giving us confidence. If we are dissatisfied with an aspect of our life and want things to be different, this image may be encouraging. Without being threatening, it offers hope, challenge and motivation.

Good examples of a first learning experience might be learning to read, ride a bicycle, play football, baking a cake. You will have your own memories.

**Prompts**

a) What have you learnt recently – or are currently learning? Notice the stages and how long it took – or is taking. Where are you on the cycle?

b) If you are helping someone with this, where do you see people getting a bit stuck?

**Ref:** David Kolb, **Experiential Learning Cycle**. 1974.

# Authenticity

## Authenticity

Are we always true to ourselves? What is our real self?

We may find we present differently to different people and in different situations. All of our ways of being may feel like the 'us' that we know and may well be appropriate for the particular occasion. This is normal.

The difficulty arises when our need for closeness leads to fitting into others' expectations of us, or we try to adapt to their ways of thinking, dressing, eating, whatever else. We can end up 'pretending' without realising. This is not very assertive. Certain situations can easily unsettle us, and, when we feel vulnerable, we put on a brave face, making out to others that we're simply fine.

If this becomes a habit, it's our false self that others see, while our real or authentic self is hidden. It's as though we sacrifice ourselves to a higher power. Put like that, we might ask – well, why would we? But it happens. And when we lose our real self, we can become frustrated and resentful without realising why. Fitting in becomes more difficult for the sake of perceived closeness.

Incidentally, children always pick up on moments when adults are not being entirely truthful or their genuine selves. They may be uneasy, using delaying tactics or avoiding eye contact; these behaviours do not go unnoticed by our children and are picked up subliminally by babies from birth.

**Prompts**

a) Try to be aware and recognise how you're coming across to others in different situations. How many different 'presences' do you have?

b) How true to yourself are you? Do you manage to speak your mind in an appropriate way? When you don't, what does it feel like?

# I'm OK, I'm not OK

Many of us are affected by the weather – and light. When the sun shines, we feel invigorated; we have more energy, our mood lifts and we feel generally more positive; bright, eager, enthusiastic, motivated. And, because positivity in one aspect of our life tends to spill over to others, this general good feeling gives us confidence. This in turn brings us competence. It's a win-win situation. Confidence and competence thrive on each other.

When it's dull, the light is poor, with or without bad weather, we can easily feel low, or maybe even lethargic, listless, unmotivated. We say, 'out of sorts'. Some of us are so sensitive to light that without sufficient brightness we don't function well; we feel sad, listless, lacking in energy and motivation. And this feeling can pervade all we do, potentially affecting those around us too.

**Prompts**

In either case, how we feel is bound to affect us one way or another. And how we feel will have an impact on those close to and around us.

a) Become aware of your moods. See if you can tell what triggers them. Less easy but enlightening: try and notice the effect your moods have on others.

b) Notice others' moods, and how they affect you.

**Eric Berne,** 1985. **Games People Play: The psychology of human relationships.** Penguin. ISBN: 0-14-00-2768-8.

## Hedgehog

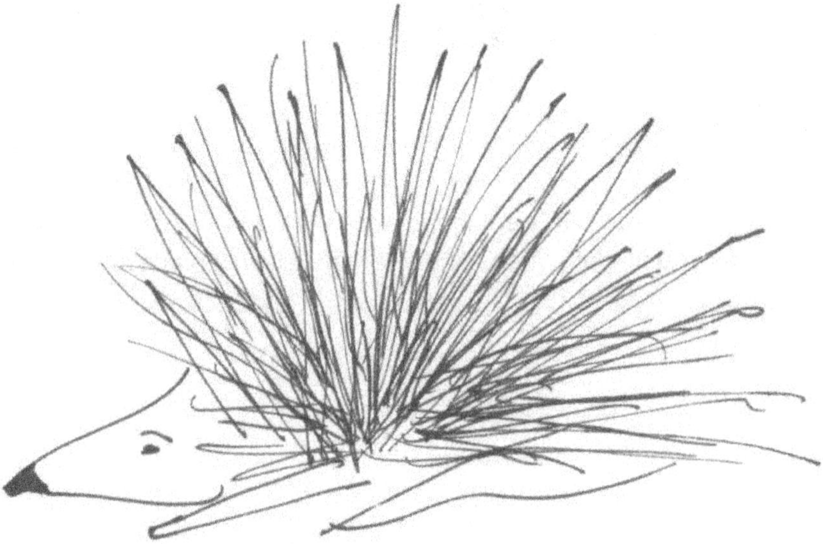

My prickles protect me
No one will want to come
near me.
I make sure of that.
And yes, I may be sulking

## Hedgehog

When we're feeling vulnerable and anxious, we're liable to become over-sensitive and fearful. We may be seen as prickly, and people may worry about upsetting us. Our prickliness is our defence; we're self-protecting; we keep others at bay.

The chances are we're feeling shy, self-conscious, unconfident, a bit got at. We might be frightened; worried about how others see us. We don't want to risk criticism, teasing or mockery. Best to stay quiet and untouchable.

This reaction, understandable though it is, acts against us. Our low mood is prolonged, if not made worse. This is the opposite of what we need and invites the saying 'we're our own worst enemy'.

**Prompts**

a) What would happen if you were to draw in your prickles? What's the smallest, simplest thing you could say to make this happen? Think of a typical situation; how could you be less prickly?

b) Try this when the next opportunity arises. What happens to you? How do others react? Do they even notice?

# Autonomy

## Status and control

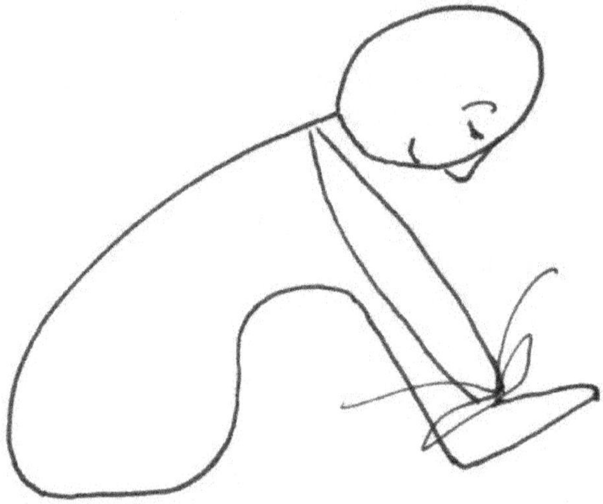

I can tie my own shoe-
laces thank you!

## Autonomy

### Status and control

Autonomy is about making decisions for yourself, being in charge of your behaviour and your actions. It means you are the agent of how and what you do, and how you respond to others. With this come good self-esteem and a strong self-image. It is about feeling competent at what we do and feeling generally on top of things.

This gives us status which we all need in our social, work and family circles. It doesn't mean we're bossy or dominating; it simply means we're holding our own assertively on a level with everyone.

Autonomy also implies a certain self-sufficiency, an independence which enhances, rather than rejects, our relationships. It also invites respect; another element important for our 'ego' – our sense of self.

What can go wrong is when we go along with what others want us to do, allowing ourselves to be led and directed by others, fitting in because it becomes easier; all this can leave us feeling useless, inept, pathetic. When we get over-ruled, when people do things for us instead of allowing us to make mistakes, we lose confidence and learn to rely on others.

**Prompts**

a) How independent are you? How does it feel? Find an example where you felt strong, confident, and autonomous.

b) In what ways do you feel dependant in some way? How does that feel? In what circumstances? And what might you do to be less so?

# Wrong fit

Here I have
room to
breathe.
I function
well.
I feel free. I am healthy

Here I am, stretched
and bound in ways
which prevent me
from functioning
well, or as I want.
I feel trapped.
I can't breathe.

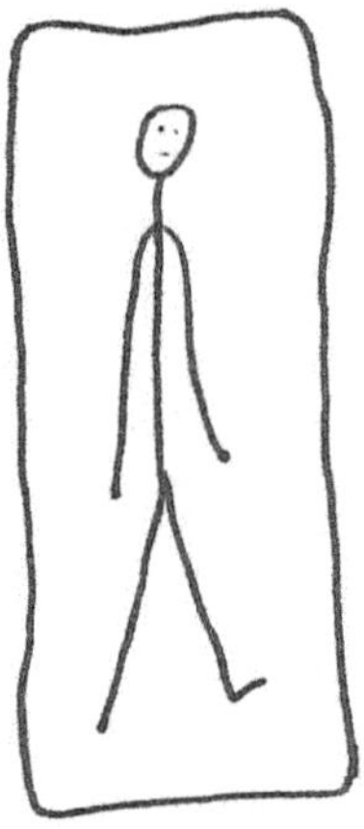

## Wrong fit

We feel comfortable being a certain way; free to love, like, think, choose, and free to behave within accepted boundaries. We know where we are and feel good about ourselves and our surroundings. In this way we are healthy in body and mind.

When others have expectations of us, make assumptions; when they make decisions for us based on their wishes and hopes – not ours – we are confused; we feel resentful and frustrated, but possibly too unassertive or even too frightened to express those feelings.

We cannot function properly when what others want of us does not match our needs, conscious or unconscious. It is a form of bullying, and we are stressed. They want us to fit into their ideas, their mould. We feel constrained, restricted, hemmed in. We are uncomfortable; frustrated, angry and helpless.

**Prompts**

If this feels like you, recognising this misfit is the first thing. Perhaps, in going along with the ways, wishes and values of others, you have lost sight of your authentic 'normal' self.

a) Acknowledge the misfit and check your position. Find a way to assert yourself, making it clear that their normal is not yours.

b) If that seems too difficult at the moment, think how you can best manage your situation until such time as you can act.

# Locked away

Stay away – I'm fine
(I'm not)
No need to visit, I'm busy
Mind your own business
Anyway, you wouldn't
understand

## Locked away

We lock our feelings and memories away for a reason, known or unknown to us. We nurture them there, knowingly, or unknowingly so they are safely hidden from the world. And hopefully from us. Unfortunately, obsessions, phobias, shame and hurt tend to fester unless attended to. We think they're well hidden, but in fact they block our path.

This is a case of our emotional brain hijacking our thinking, and we believe our secret is safe from ourselves. However, it's a fact that keeping a secret or holding on to a ritual or a grudge, for example, is like carrying heavy baggage – emotional baggage. This uses up a lot of energy which could be put to better use with more open and positive preoccupations.

**Prompts**

a) Take the 'key' to unlock your brain and engage your thinking brain. Find something you really would prefer not to dwell on anymore and simply **think** a positive thought to replace the shameful one. This takes time; be patient with yourself.

b) If you can manage this change, note your surprise and pleasure and 'clock' your success.

# Emotional bin

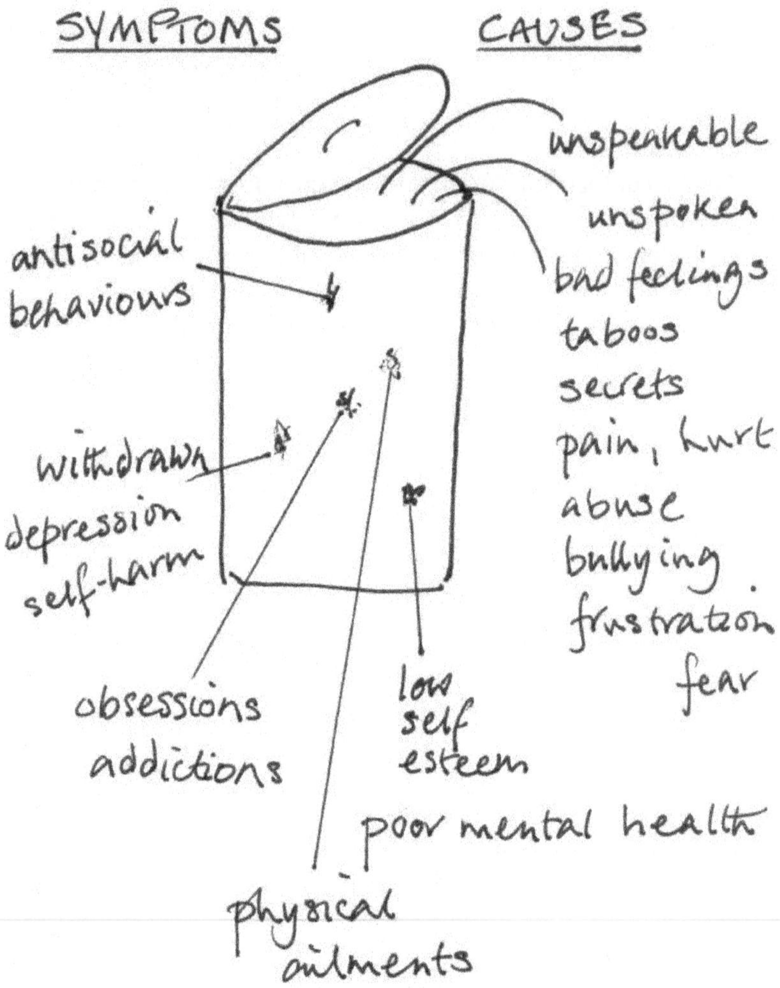

## Emotional bin

One way of understanding our behaviour and emotions is to make the link between past experiences and how we are today; our learning, if you like, or rather what we have been taught. The bin represents the metaphorical dark place where the years of secrets, lies and taboos accumulated from childhood are stashed away, hidden from our conscious self, the lid shut firmly down. The bin provides a safe place to store difficult thoughts and feelings, for example bad memories, fears, guilt, anger, jealousy. All that is unspeakable and unspoken is rammed in, out of consciousness, until the bin can take in no more.

The individual items which went in at the top are no longer recognisable. All the bad stuff mixes and mingles as it churns around inside. The accumulation of repressed bottled-up feelings fills the bin to bursting point. The bin has a finite volume and begins to show signs of stress. Our stress is expressed in unhealthy and antisocial behaviours.

### Prompts

Just dealing with the symptoms, the current behaviours, is not enough; it's what went in that needs to be addressed. Ignoring the root cause is like putting a plaster on a deep wound that first needs cleaning before it can begin to heal.

a) Don't be afraid of lifting the lid. You may need someone to help you look inside. Start exploring with the support of someone who you know will understand.

b) It's important that you begin to accept your bin's contents; with support you can forgive yourself and others about what happened in the past which you needed to stuff in your bin.

# Buried Shame

Can we really walk away

from what we think we have buried?

## Buried shame

Here is another metaphor for putting aside thoughts and feelings, or memories, which cause us pain and shame. Shame – or a self-conscious embarrassment – can arise in any of us about all sorts of stuff; this stuff usually includes a sense of inadequacy, either about past situations and circumstances which seem to haunt us, or in the here and now, today.

Something I call 'negative comparison' is often at work here. It seems a common feature of being human to compare ourselves negatively with others and so feel relatively small and insignificant. Envy or, stronger, jealousy, can do this.

If we are sensitive to criticism and teasing; if we feel maltreated or even misunderstood; if we have suffered abuse or neglect in any form; if as a child we had no defence and were made to feel we were to blame; if we look back and review an event where we made a mistake, got it wrong, felt 'shown up'…. all these examples, and more, would induce a sense of not being good enough. Shame is at the extreme end of the spectrum. We may grow up feeling guilty and that we deserve to be punished.

**Prompts**

a) If you think you have some buried shame, take a mental look at one event where you find it still very difficult to go, in your head. Be brave and ask yourself whether you have cause to be ashamed now, today. Talk it through with someone who will help you see things more objectively.

b) Pass it back mentally to where it belongs. Acknowledge its origin; where did it come from? Who told you this, did this to you? Etc.

# Notice Me!

Paradoxically, those who behave like this in fact probably have a sense of deep-seated insecurity.

We like to be recognised; we need to belong and be respected. Admittedly, respect is earned, and, once we have this, we have status within our groups, whether social, family, work or other. Without status we are missing something, our self-image suffers.

Status helps us to feel confident; we're more likely to respond to challenges, feel in control and work competently towards a goal and a sense of achievement.

And yet, if for some reason we need more attention than we already have (we can't get enough of it), we feel the urge to elbow our way to the front regardless of those around us, pushing our way through.

**Prompts**

a) What groups do you belong to? Note how your sense of status may differ depending on the group, and whether sometimes you find yourself elbowing your way to the front.

b) How do you react when you see this elbowing behaviour? What do you think is driving this person?

# Throwing the toys out of the pram

## Throwing the toys out of the pram

This image makes me smile. A child has a tantrum because they can't get their own way. If this continues into adulthood, we have someone with whom it is almost impossible to have a rational, level discussion, or where we might each take our turn to put our point of view and be heard. With this person there's no chance. They therefore lose friends and then blame the ex-friends for the break-up. They are very lonely; they cannot seem to take responsibility for their actions, always finding others to blame. And yet they can gather around them a loyal (and scared?) group of hangers-on, thus appearing to be in charge. They aren't of course, but in these circumstances, they control by subtle bullying.

We can all feel like chucking it all in sometimes (or out as in this case). It's an impulse, when we're frustrated (can't get our own way) and feel the other isn't paying us due attention. However, the less egoistic of us will be able to pause, pull back and see the point of rational dialogue. There is little chance that such a narcissistic person will change.

**Prompts**

a) Do you know someone who is on this spectrum – expects to be indulged, is so self-absorbed they're unaware of others? How do you react? How do you feel and what do you do?

b) Maybe you see yourself as somewhere on this line, in which case ask others for helpful observations. Be brave and seek constructive feedback from someone you trust.

# Our different parts

## Our different parts

Sometimes we find ourselves behaving in ways we didn't expect, and we don't like it. Or wishing we hadn't said something. How come we're so taken by surprise?

It can be useful to think of our personality as made up of several parts; and unsettling when we discover that we don't really like some of them.

Let's take for example three main basic characteristics as identified by Eric Berne which exist in us as 'states'; the child, the parent and the adult. Each of these can take over our personality according to the situation that challenges us in the moment. We will all have something in our childhood where we were treated unkindly or thoughtlessly or at least in any way that ignored, denied or dismissed our essential needs for security and trust. It only needs a trigger to let out the 'child' part of us, whether it be frightened, temperamental, rebellious, sullen, demanding...

As for the parent state, we learn from our own parents and significant others how they treat people, and we follow suit, absorbing as we grow up how we have experienced parental behaviour and attitudes, naturally imitating them. When our 'parent' takes over, we can be loving and caring, as well as authoritarian and critical.

The 'adult' state is the one where we feel more balanced.

**Prompts**

a) How often, in what situations and with whom do you recognise any of these 'states' in your behaviour?

b) Observe others' behaviour and note if you can the 'state' which has taken over.

Ref: **Eric Berne**, 1983. **The Games People Play: The psychology of human relationships.** Penguin UK, ISBN: 0-14-00-2768-8.

Regrets
That was then
This is now

## Regrets

### That was then, this is now

All too easily we can get caught up in nostalgia. 'What if' and 'If only' can become persistent plaintive cries in our head. They can take up a lot of space, more than is helpful. But what's done is done, it is said. That's all very well.

Looking back is normal. However, it can be dangerous if it holds you so strongly in the past that you find it hard to enjoy the present, particularly if it encourages negative, self-deprecating moods of blame and recrimination. Sometimes looking back on happy times makes us sad too, and that loss can cause us to feel very lonely and bereft.

More immediately, instead of wasting time and energy dwelling on a recent mistake, use your resources in the moment to do your best.

**Prompts**

a) Recall a really happy memory where you felt loved and cherished, comfortable. Keep it safe and think of it as one of the good things that influences who you are today.

b) If you find yourself dwelling on a time when you were unhappy, you felt unloved and wish things could have been different, remember **That was then, this is now** and use this memory to enrich your understanding of both yourself and others. What happened - happened. Blaming either ourselves or others does not help.

# 3-legged stool

Balance

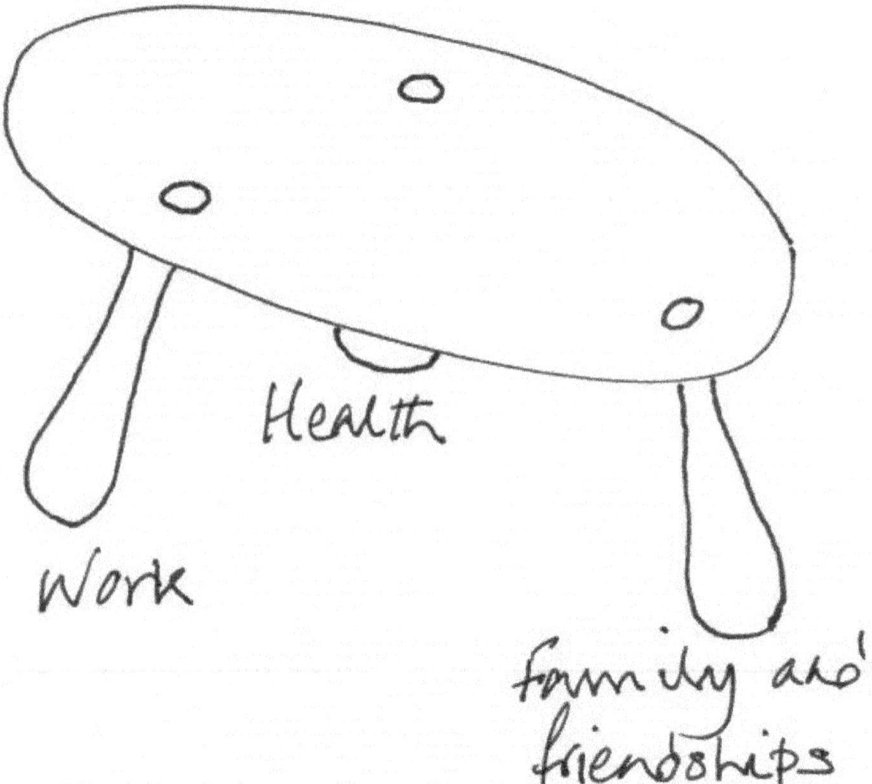

## Three-legged stool

### Balance

This analogy is applied to a whole host of aspects in our lives today. Each leg represents a vital aspect of our lives: Health, Work, Family and Friendships.

It began with the Post World War II generation planning for their retirement. The legs at that time represented Employers' pension, Employees' savings and Social Security. It is thought to have originated in a speech by Reinhard A Hohans on social security America in 1949.

This rather over-simplified idea helps us to think about balance in our life. The three legs together keep us stable. With one leg missing we would find it quite difficult to keep upright. With two legs missing – well, unless we're a trapeze artist, we're done for. And four legs won't work if the ground is uneven. We can take 'ground' to be a metaphor that suits our own situation.

I guess we take the three aspects for granted; we don't think about these if we experience all three as going well. It seems that only when we're aware that something is wrong or missing do we begin to address the balance.

**Prompts**

a) How balanced is your life? If you can identify dissatisfaction or frustration, to which leg does it belong? How might you start to change things?

b) It might be easier to draw your own pie chart with different slice sizes to see how balanced your life is.

## SECTION 2

### BLOCKS TO HEALTHY RELATIONSHIPS

What stops us doing what we want to do? Why don't we like being told what to do? And what makes us resist something really nice that we're being offered? When we feel uncomfortable and don't want to face a difficulty, a confrontation, an awkward situation, we bury our head in the sand, so we don't have to look. Incidentally, ostriches don't do this to avoid anything; they are checking their eggs buried there.

What are our avoidance strategies? Our delaying tactics? How did these come about? Where, with whom and how did we learn these tricks? What pattern are we matching?

How many displacement activities do we employ so we don't have to attend to something we don't want to deal with?

Ignorance, embarrassment, guilt, shame and fear are big drivers which block our ability to make and maintain good, balanced relationships; relationships with people, ideas, behaviours, even rules and regulations, the status quo.... All these emotional responses to stuff dominate our brain to the extent that our thinking shuts down. In the words of Human Givens author Joe Griffin 'emotional arousal makes us stupid' – which just about sums it up. Inevitably, such one-sidedness of perception is bound to affect our ability to make a decision, or to make, maintain and even to end a relationship with ease and confidence.

Equally, loss of a loved one, through illness, death, break up or other significant event; and other losses such as redundancy, moving house, loss of a friendship, losing our sense of freedom, etc., can affect us all in different ways. Reactions of course are unique to us, and can take us by surprise, not to mention to the surprise of those in our family/social circle. These blocks are a mixture of events, which we see as threatening, mainly because they're beyond our control, and the experiences which make up our lives today. There follow a few metaphors to illustrate these ideas.

# Elephant in the room

I am enormous. I take up
a lot of space in the room
– emotional space

## Elephant in the room

Most of us will have experienced a time when something is not being said. This image represents a huge impediment to a real conversation about stuff that's important.

We may know what's not being addressed and be part of the unspoken conspiracy. It may be that both or all of us know what it is that's being avoided. No-one dares bring up the unmentionable for fear of upset; and upset will be too difficult to deal with. So, we leave the elephant where it is.

Or we get a sense of something that's not quite right, something uncomfortable in the air, but have no idea what it is. Conversation in these circumstances can be awkward, to say the least.

**Prompts**

a) If you find yourself caught up in the avoidance conspiracy, be brave and acknowledge what it is that's not being mentioned. You want the matter freely discussed and out in the open. Feel the relief when you challenge in this way.

b) If you're feeling uncomfortable about something you don't understand, take a risk and ask what's going on.

# Walking on eggshells

With some people we feel we have to go very carefully so as not to cause upset, or "rock the boat" - another metaphor.

## Walking on eggshells

This is how it can feel when we're trying very hard not to upset anybody; and when we want to make sure we are acceptable – and accepted. We do not say what is in our mind to say. When we're afraid to challenge someone's behaviour or opinion, for example, or afraid to speak our mind, it is usually for fear of rejection or being the butt of the other's anger or frustration, or even criticism or derision. The trouble is, while avoiding such potential difficulties, the business between us is unfinished and nothing is sorted; the unspoken comment can fester in us, and the other is none the wiser about the effect their behaviour has had.

This way of being over-careful in what we perceive to be a tricky situation can be uncomfortable at best and certainly not helpful to either party. Depending on the degree of frustration we feel, it may well involve us in pretending, not being true to ourselves. And this, surprisingly, takes up more emotional energy than being real. What a waste of energy!

Prompts

a) Ask yourself why you're working so hard to protect others – and therefore you – from potential upset. How did this start? And with whom?

b) What would happen if you spoke your mind? If you take the risk, note the effect of this on everyone involved. And congratulate yourself on an important step to authenticity.

Buttoned - up

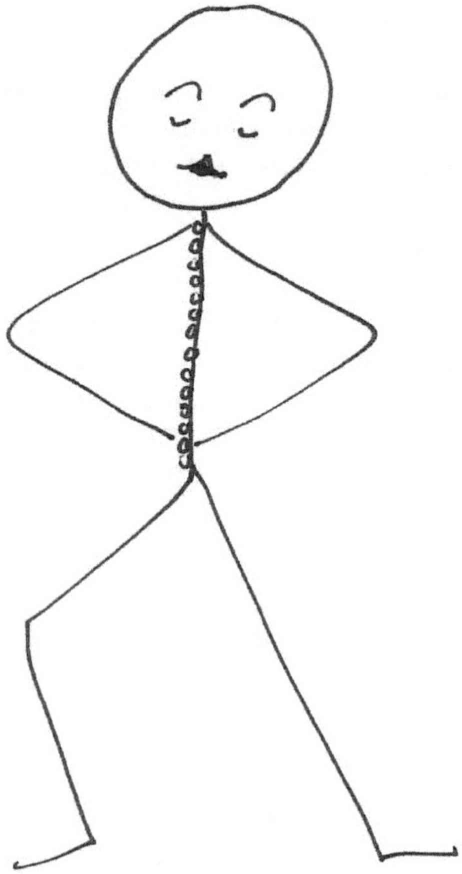

## Buttoned up

Here is another expression we have for hiding away thoughts and feelings we don't want to deal with. We want to get on with life, pretending everything is fine. Appearances are what matter; we expect others to accept this surface presence. Our true feelings as well as the difficult stuff are securely stored behind the stiffly buttoned up jacket.

This way we're protecting ourselves from hurt by presenting a false and brittle front, buttoning up our unspoken fears and needs.

Of course, there comes a time when we have got so used to hiding our real self that others know us only as our false self. Which means our real self remains needful of attention and response.

**Prompts**

a) Imagine the buttons are being stretched to the point of breaking off. Would you want to prevent this? And to keep the buttons in place? Or to keep your true self safe from prying?

b) What might be held tight behind those buttons? Find one thing in there which you might be brave enough to take out and show the world, or at least someone close to you.

# Claws

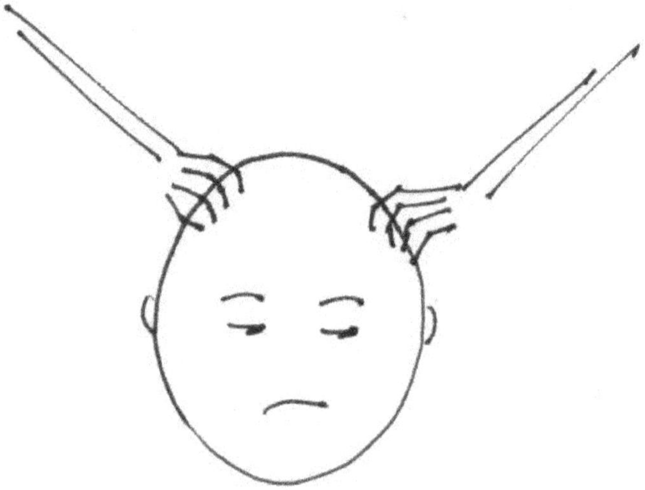

When an obsession takes hold it's as though we're in the clutches of a great strong bird of prey with huge claws. They cling, they dig in. We feel helpless, unable to free ourselves

## Claws

There can be times when our mind is so fixed on something that there seems to be no room for anything else. Our power, our autonomy, has been taken away as the obsession takes hold.

When this happens it's as though we're in the clutches of a great strong bird of prey. Their claws cling. They dig in. We feel helpless, unable to be free. Fear takes over and we can't think properly. A good example of how emotion can hijack our thinking.

**Prompts**

a) If it helps, imagine the bird on your head holding on aggressively. Try in your mind unbending the finger of each claw one by one. Gradually you will begin to take control and you can begin to feel freer.

b) While doing this you could repeat "Let go!" or something more polite, or even more rude, giving it a firm and confident message. Think of one that suits you.

The secret here is to think and so **feel** confident, so some practice may be needed. Find your own way to talk to it. You will begin to feel it separating from you.

# Resistance

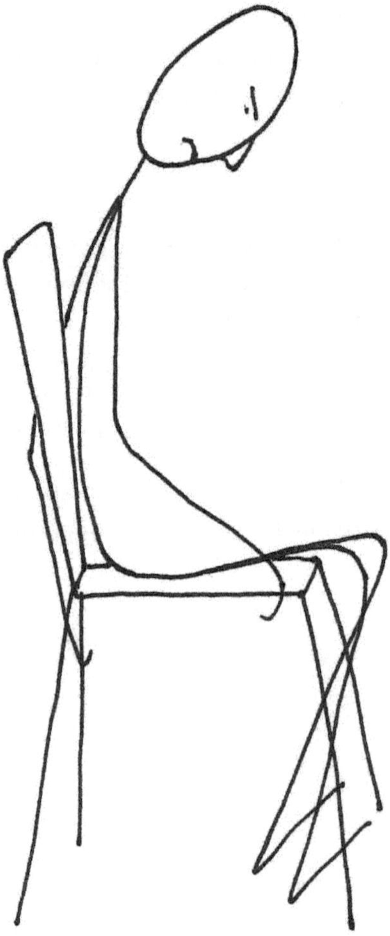

## Resistance

When we feel bombarded by family and friends with advice, commands, and expectations, telling us or implying what we ought to do, how to do it and more, our response is usually not to receive it either gratefully or graciously! Indeed, when expectations of us are covert and unspoken – in other words we pick this up somehow, sense it – we tend to retreat mentally if not obviously and physically. While the advice, or whatever pressure it is, is meant to encourage, it has in fact the opposite effect: it discourages. It's strange that this is not understood by the person with expectations, trying to help us by giving advice.

Feeling discouraged, our self-esteem, our sense of self, crumbles; it is already at a low ebb. We rebel. We dig in our heels, defiant and defensive. Rather than engaging in conversation assertively, we clam up (another metaphor!), feeling criticised and judged. And this is the mood which causes us to be defensive.

In order to avoid this, 'fogging' is a way of describing how to deal with unhelpful remarks. For example: "I need some time to think about that". Alternatively, if it fits, a simple, brief response as in "You may be right" or a straight-forward "You're wrong here" can put off our aggressor and go towards regaining our real self.

**Prompts**

a) How do you deal with unhelpful advice? Or being told what would be best for you? If you can remember a time when this happened, how did you feel and what did you do? What might you try now?

b) Notice when others get defensive. How do you know? And what triggered it? Consider whether you feel 'fogged'.

Pandora's box

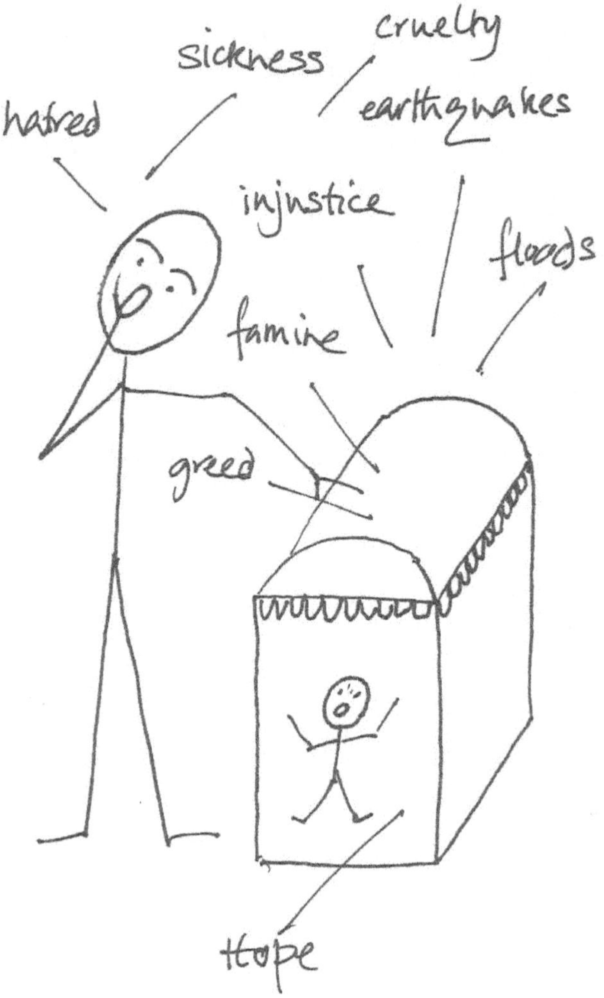

## Pandora's box

This is the box in Greek mythology allegedly presented in revenge to Pandora by Zeus. Who opened it is not clear, but when it was, out flew all the evils of humanity into the world. The story goes that she slammed the lid down – presumably in horror – thus trapping inside the one thing that could have made things better, hope. Unsurprisingly, it is a woman (Pandora or A. N. Other), who is blamed for the evil in the world. And for leaving hope behind.

What pessimistic doom and gloom! Legends are full of explanations as to why life is the way it is. When we say: I don't want to open Pandora's box, we could also say a 'can of worms' because we don't want to have to deal with the worms. We dare not do this, say that, try another, for fear of something terrible happening. One word for this is 'catastrophising'. In other words, expecting the worst, we avoid it – to our detriment.

Now, if in the past we have experienced 'the worst' in our eyes, then it's perfectly understandable that we expect more 'worst' to happen. It's hard to believe it won't. This way of seeing our world holds us back.

**Prompts**

a) What might be in your Pandora's box? What do you fear might happen?

b) Try to imagine opening it to release Hope (and Hope's friends) that got left behind.

# Anxiety blocks performance 1

To Do List

Contact bank re statement
Deep clean oven
Check emails
M.O.T
Buy cat food
Tidy room
Put out bins
Groceries
Visit...
Ring...
New list
Renew house insurance
. . .

## Anxiety blocks performance 1

We can often feel stressed by the sheer number of tasks awaiting our attention. We may feel unable to address any of them, not knowing where to start. This list is too long! We can be stunned into inertia. We may find 'displacement' activities to keep us occupied.... so, we feel OK putting off dealing with the items on the list. We procrastinate.

In this way our anxiety is increased. Something needs to happen. The nearer the deadline, the more intense is the anxiety. We need to take it in stages, one step at a time, not worrying about the next thing.

Who has never been bounced into a decision we later regret? We were not ready for the choices and felt pressured to decide in the moment. This is a common example of how our feelings of mild panic take over our thinking. We need time to make a sensible and relevant decision; this can feel crucial, and yet too much time can be confusing. We are so emotionally aroused that we cannot think. And yes, we may describe ourselves as stupid in that situation.

**Prompts**

a) To avoid procrastination, you may find listing your tasks in priority order helpful, according to the relative urgency as you see it. Be realistic; and ticking them off as you complete a task can be encouraging. A sense of achievement is vital when we're feeling low.

b) Or get a large sheet of paper and draw a web of lots of clouds. Each cloud represents a task needing attention. You can then choose according to your preference, your mood, your sense of urgency.

Anxiety blocks performance 2

## Anxiety blocks performance 2

When we feel overwhelmed with fears, confronted with more to do or to be responsible for than seems possible; when we're stressed to the point of feeling inadequate or incompetent; it is at this point that our anxiety seems to have taken over our whole self, to have taken hold to such an extent that we cease to function properly. We lose things, forget stuff, drop things, put stuff away in the wrong place.... This is a classic case of the emotional brain hijacking the thinking brain.

Anxiety can lead to obsessive thoughts and behaviours, as though we're in control. In fact, we're not in control; rather we're captive to their control. We feel powerful yet powerless. Our anxiety has taken over, has become a familiar habit too hard to break. We might even say, bewildered and frustrated, 'I've been here before!'

One way of dealing with our anxiety, and freeing ourselves of it, is to think of it as a separate entity. The phrase 'I was beside myself' comes to mind. So, try this.

**Prompts**

a) Imagine your anxiety in a chair opposite, or beside you, and having a conversation with it. Give it a name. Could you describe it? Give it a form, an identity, if you like. Imagine asking what it wants, why it's plaguing you. Put yourself in its shoes and try to answer the questions. You may find you're able to answer. This strange exercise can be quite an eye-opener.

b) Another way of exploring this would be to get a good friend (a very good friend) to play one of the parts – you or your anxiety.

# Emotionally disabled 1

My heart is broken

I'm unreliable
I'm not with you

## Emotionally disabled 1

We are all (dis)abled in our own way, and our responses to grief are unique to us.

When grief takes us by surprise, or another shocking event we're not prepared for, or when a number of bad things have happened or seem to be happening to us all at once.... it can be really hard to be sensitive to the loss or disappointment of others, or indeed to take an interest in anything or anyone else. Our grief tends to leave other emotions out, and can be as all-consuming as anxiety, in that we feel very alone; we are abandoned. However kind and thoughtful are the people around us, we are literally un-comfortable. Feeling 'disabled' in this way, we are unable to be actively there for others. At the same time, we feel that no-one can possibly be there for us.

And just as we feel isolated, so it is with others who are equally suffering. Paradoxically, while we feel unable to connect emotionally to others when in this state, this is exactly the time, the moment, when we need this connection. We may appear to reject the love and support we are offered, in spite of how much we need and crave it.

**Prompts**

a) Allow yourself to acknowledge, if not express, your feelings; do not pretend you're fine when you are not. There will be moments in your life when it is important to put yourself truly first. This may be one of them. Recognise and explain as best you can your need to be 'selfish', i.e., try to take care of yourself with what you need.

b) Ask others to be kind and available, and not tell you to 'get over it'. Suggest they avoid words such as 'should' and 'ought'.

**NB:** Emotionally disabled 2 in section 5.

# Grieving 1

I am my grief
I can't believe things
will ever be different

## Grieving 1

One way of understanding our grief and the pain it brings is to feel it as all-consuming. Newly bereaved, our grief fills our life. It takes up all our energy and attention, all our mental and emotional space. **It is us; we are it**. We find it almost impossible to think about anything else. The rest of life holds little interest for us. We can't sleep, don't want to eat, find inappropriate coping strategies. Our tired and under-nourished brain finds it difficult to focus. With time it will begin to take up less relative space, but right now there is room for little else.

The grief of bereavement – and indeed of any significant loss – can eat us up. For a while, all else is neglected. How long this 'while' is depends entirely on the circumstances - our personality, our way of responding to loss and the kind of support available to us at the time.

The stress will take its toll, so we need to look after ourselves by allowing others around us to be supportive. We may notice physical symptoms such as headaches, stomach aches, sleeplessness, nausea, or whatever we're prone to when anxiety hits.

**Prompts**

a) What was your most recent loss? How did you react? What physical symptoms did you suffer? And how long before you felt more able to focus on the rest of life again?

b) How do you feel when someone you know is grieving a significant loss? What happens to you then?

# Grieving 2

Fried egg theory

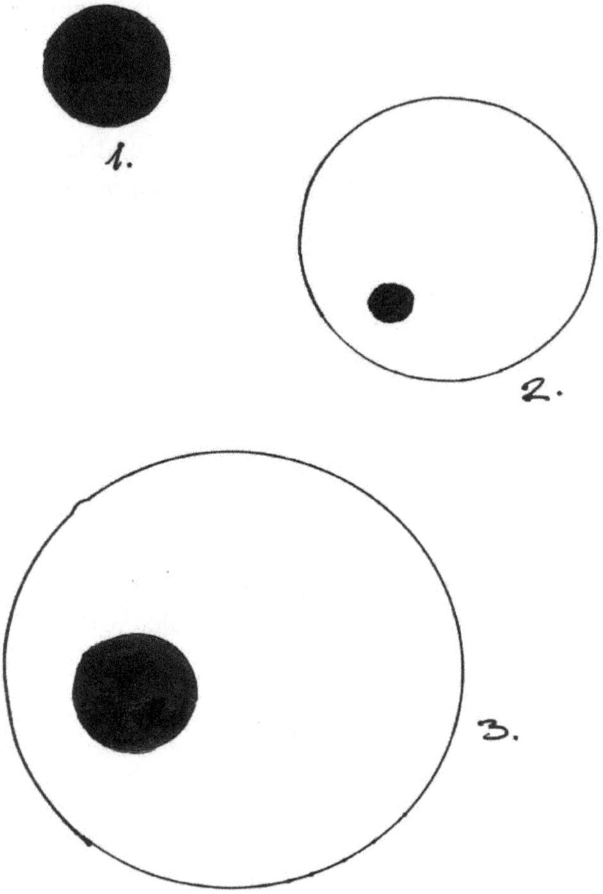

## Grieving 2

### Fried egg theory

It was years ago that a student came up with the idea of the fried egg. During a grief workshop in New Zealand, which she attended after the death of her child, she described her experiences of bereavement.

She recognised that her grief had entirely enveloped her to start with (see Figure 1). And then, with time, she felt that her grief was no longer taking up all her life. Realising that it would never entirely go away, she envisaged it permanently with her but no longer blocking out the rest of her life. She could begin to spread out, carrying her sadness lovingly with her while getting on with her life. Hence the fried egg image, the grief the yolk and her life the egg white. Unexpectedly, it didn't get any smaller (see Figure 2).

Instead, she realised that her grief remained as large as ever, and that our grief stays with us, while our life begins to expand around it (see Figure 3). Although at times of anniversaries and other reminders, our sadness may well up again and take up a bit more space, nevertheless, with more emotional and mental space, we shall increasingly experience life around us; and be the richer for it.

**Prompts**

a) How does this image resonate with you? How is the life-space around your grief?

b) How could you best support someone who is grieving?

**Ref: Fried Egg Theory.** Adapted from **Bereavement Care Journal,** Spring 1996.

# SECTION 3

## INFLUENCES FROM THE PAST

If yesterday keeps getting in the way of today, then moving forward into tomorrow may be difficult.

It can be useful to see our present difficulties or issues as connected somehow to the past. This is pattern-matching. When we notice that our current behaviours and attitudes are holding us back, and it seems familiar.......

It cannot be ignored that we are today the entire sum of our experiences from the earliest moments since our birth; some would say since our conception. More than the sum, we are the result of all the consequences of those experiences. It is all of this that makes us who we are today. And given that we are a link in our generation chain, we inevitably carry family experiences with us as we develop.

The familiar 'nature/nurture' aspect of our personality is highly relevant to the way we live, think, feel, and behave. The more we can learn about ourselves and our family history, the more likely we shall grow up strong and healthy in mind and body and less prone to become victims of any previous family trauma. Let us rather be pro-active than re-active.

Nature is about what we're born with, all those qualities such as intelligence, innate skills, memory, imagination, empathy, etc. along with the significant needs such as being loved and attended to, security, autonomy, intimacy, companionship, etc. These are the Human Givens which underpin our existence; our healthy functioning depends on all our needs being sufficiently met in order to be in a good state to use our resources.

Nurture on the other hand is all the rest that we've taken in along the way. Our first learning comes from responding to others' ways of being with us and how we are treated by them, and of course by imitation. And straight away we're sucked into the family culture and the family ways of doing things. Just as we may look like our family members physically, with many of their facial expressions, gestures, mannerisms, so may we inherit likes and dislikes, habits, and behaviours.

It is suggested that 25% of people exposed to traumatic events develop PTSD (Griffin and Tyrrell 2013) in later life. Put as simply as possible, when an event triggers a memory, thus causing heightened stress, emotional pattern-matching comes into play. Different elements in the brain are unable to make the logical connection between yesterday and today, and the victim is caught up in the trauma as if it were happening again today.

It is clear from the ideas that follow how easily we can be affected as we grow up by past experiences and the inevitable learning.

**Ref: Wilson J P, Keane T M**, 1997. Assessing psychological trauma and PTSD, in **Griffin J, Tyrell I**, 2013. Human Givens, a new approach to emotional health and clear thinking. ISBN: 1-899-398-26-0.

# Waterfall of love 1.

## The flow of unconditional love

### Waterfall of love 1

Our past has a complex relationship with our present. We think of love, care and responsibility flowing freely like a river from our parents down to us, their children, then from us as adults to our children, from them to theirs and so on through the generations. This flow of love is the basis of our healthy development – emotional, mental, physical; it's all as one. As children we absorb emotionally not only the way our family relationships play out, but also how previous generations have managed their reactions to events in their lives.

A parent's job, their responsibility, is to love, nurture and cherish their children. And it is the children's 'job' to receive all this; use it to their advantage and pass it on when the time comes, as parents to their children. And so on.

As parents, we do the best we can in the circumstances in which we find ourselves, and with the legacy of our parents' experiences and how they brought us up. For how we are cared for as children stays with us through our lives and influences how we bring up our children, and indeed how we see and behave with others.

**Prompts**

a) Perhaps you have become aware of the love flowing in your family, and as a result what you have to give and to pass on to others. Note what aspects of your parents, grandparents, or other relatives have become part of who you are. What have you picked up or inherited?

b) How have these aspects affected or influenced you or your children's personalities, mannerisms, abilities, etc?

# Waterfall of love 2

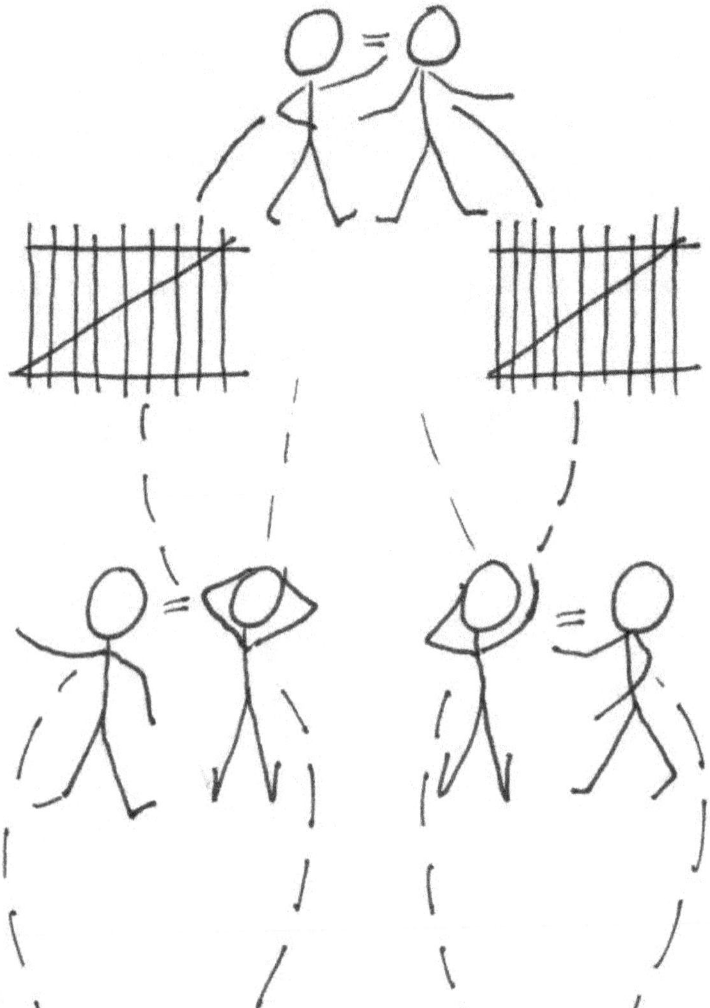

## The flow of unconditional love

## Waterfall of love 2

If a parent's loving feelings are constricted, it's most likely because that parent has suffered deep hurt or sadness sometime in their own upbringing. It may be that a parent's love flow hits a barrier along the way. This could happen to any of us. Unforeseen events, unexpected circumstances beyond our control can visit upon us any time and will present barriers to our healthy development. We deal with them as best we can, as seems the only thing to do at the time.

If as parents such occurrences are too difficult for us to manage, and the stress levels are too high to function well, it is left to our children to try and manage for us. Thus, as children our roles are reversed. Instead of looking forward and on, developing through our childhood with the love and nurture we need from our parents, our progress is halted. We find ourselves wading up-stream, with concern and worry and, yes, feeling responsible for their well-being.

In this way, paradoxically, by looking back we are shoved forward into an adulthood filled with a responsibility for which we are not ready. From needing care and nourishment for all our senses and attributes from our parents, we become their carers of sorts, as best we can; confused, possibly frightened, inevitably also struggling. Stress levels remain high; resentment, anger or simply confusion can lead us to blame ourselves for what went wrong, and for our perceived inadequacy.

If our family system is stressed in any way, we will absorb the negative vibes flowing down the generations, learning self-protective behaviours: shutting out reality, pleasing people, retreating into ourselves or cutting off from those close to us. This carries on into adult life, our uncherished child still with us.

**Prompts**

a) If this situation resonates with you, it might be interesting to look back through the generations in your family. You might find out about events in the lives of your forebears which you now see have to some extent disrupted the healthy flow of love.

b) No-one is to blame for circumstances diverting the flow. Understanding and compassion are called for here. You may like some help to talk it through and explore your findings and reactions.

# Living with the tyranny of the past

## Living with the tyranny of the past

## That was then, this is now

When we feel we can't handle a situation or we're frightened of embarking on a task, or feel frustrated, incomprehensibly stuck.... it's possible that, unconsciously, we are reminded of a past experience, an event, a moment, or an uncomfortable situation; a time when we felt inadequate, incapable, unsuited to the task; put down, shown up; in other words, where the message we received was one that confirmed how hopeless or useless we were.

I call this the tyranny of the past. It is indeed pattern-matching; it can play its part over and over again, in our present, today – if we let it. Our past has an uncanny habit of popping up when we least expect it. It is most likely that we are not aware of this as we struggle with the moment's lack of confidence and some of the accompanying physical symptoms. Such reactions can certainly hold us back. At these times we can find ourselves acting inappropriately. For example, we may feel antagonistic towards someone who presents **now**, who talks, behaves and/or looks like someone from our past, whom we feared for good reason **then**. A memory triggers in us **now** the response feelings we had **then**, which today are not relevant. Misunderstandings can all too easily arise.

### Prompts

Recalling and acknowledging what happened in the past is important because it helps to place **now** in its proper context. We should not let the past hold us or our future to ransom.

a) Remind yourself **That was then, this is now**. Or, for example, 'That was my parent, uncle, gran, teacher, etc., this is my partner, friend, etc.' The situation might feel similar, bring up unhappy memories – though as mentioned above most likely unconscious – but these are different people, different circumstances.

b) Question your reactions when such a situation arises, in other words try to work out where these feeling come from, reminding yourself that unconscious mechanisms are at work. And be in the **now**.

# Why don't you understand me?

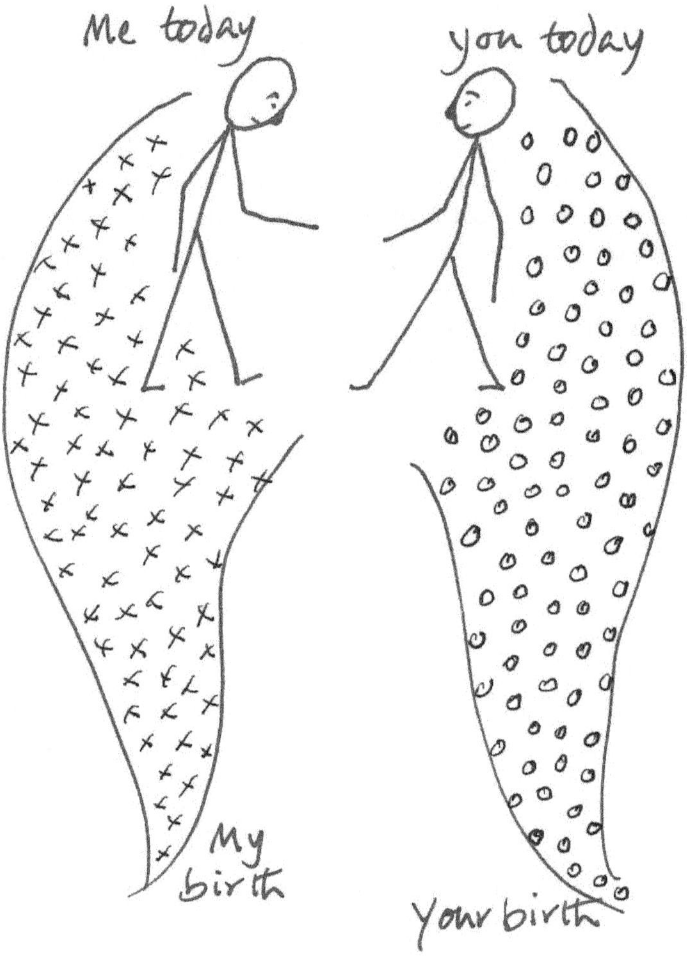

## Why don't you understand me?

We are all individuals with our own peculiarities, particularities and personal history. No two experiences are the same, in spite of the common response 'Oh yes, the exact same thing happened to me!' We are of course made up of the sum of all our own life experiences to date, and they are unique to us. Our family, our culture, the environment where we were brought up and educated, the relationships we formed, etc. – all of these and more inform our expectations of ourselves and others. They tell us also how things should be done and what is important to us.

As a result, we're bound to view and react to the world in ways which make sense uniquely to us and which reinforce our sense of self in it. Inevitably this can lead to misunderstandings. It's no wonder therefore that we get confused or upset – or even mystified - when others don't share our ideas, opinions or the 'right' way to do things. Others' expectations can feel a burden when they are not our own. Misunderstandings and miscommunication can easily occur.

And since no two experiences can ever be the same – similar, yes, but never the exact same – situations or incidents which we experience might well resonate with others but cannot belong to them. Connections are made, we make comparisons, we share our own and marvel sometimes at their similarity or difference. There is a call here for tolerance, understanding and compassion as well as celebration for all our differences.

**Prompts**

It's often comforting to recognise similarities. It's also important to acknowledge the differences and how we react to them.

a) What role does miscommunication play in your relationships? How do you handle differences?

b) To what extent are you open-minded about other people's expectations of you?

# Baggage 1

sometimes
we feel as
though
we're too burdened to
carry on

## Baggage 1

If we feel overwhelmed in a way that holds us back; if we feel burdened with more than we can cope with; when we feel our goodwill is being abused, and we are taken for granted.... We are stuck emotionally somewhere unpleasant and feel unable to find a way out. We can get into a rut as a habit builds up of helping people out, or attending to others, until we're exhausted. We begin to feel inadequate, that we can't manage, but carry on regardless. Somehow, we have learned to respond to others' needs in this way. Where did we learn to be like this? Who else in our family...? Etc.

We may feel so burdened that it is almost impossible to have a fulfilling, equal and level relationship with another. In fact, we may keep trying to make friends, to become close or intimate, but fail to maintain this for any length of time. For some reason we often don't understand, the relationship peters out.

Unless we can resolve this in some way, we tend to launch ourselves into relationships that don't work for us. We tend to hang on until something in us snaps; we come to understand the destructive power of the baggage-carrying habit and the dysfunctional nature of the relationship.

**Prompts**

a) How have you become such a burdened person? What influences can you identify that got you to this stressful place?

b) If you can separate the different aspects of your baggage, what do you see?

# Baggage 2

. . . and yet we can find ourselves offering to take on even more. Such generosity may appear to help the other person. It certainly will not benefit you.

## Baggage 2

It may be that we are so used to carrying a lot of emotional weight that we are no longer aware of it, since it has been with us as long as we can remember. For example, if we grew up with a lot of responsibility due to family circumstances, such as coping with younger siblings if our parents were out of action for some reason, this way of being remains with us. We carry it into adulthood almost unawares because it's a significant part of who we have become.

It may be that we experienced a troubled childhood when circumstances prevented us from being authentic or deprived us of unconditional love; or when secrets were rife. With more responsibility than we feel we can cope with we continue to carry it all without question or good management. We stop functioning well and our thinking becomes blocked. As we continue in the role of burden-carrier, we even offer to take on more! The danger is we could become a burden to others, but this is hard for us to see.

**Prompts**

a) Recognise your limits and be respectful of boundaries: what you can and will take on, and what you know you cannot and should not, and therefore will not take on. Start with something small.

b) Try not to feel responsible for others' burdens, because in fact you are not. Listen and support without allowing yourself to be dumped on. You have your own stuff to look out for.

# Coping strategies 1

more alcohol than is good for us

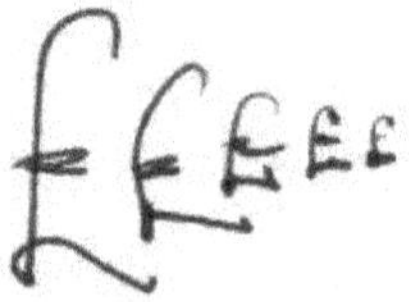

gambling

smoking drugs

more food than we need

over-working

## Coping strategies 1

When under mental or emotional stress it's easy to fall into comfort-zone habits. These are not necessarily healthy. Some of these might be labelled self-harming. 'I need a drink' is not infrequently heard when in shock, for example. Not that having a drink per se is necessarily harmful. It's the extent, frequency and seemingly uncontrollability of the habit that gets us into trouble. It can be so easy to slip into the habitual responses when things seem so tough.

Paradoxically, what we really need at a crisis point are health-promoting activities and behaviours which will both keep us going physically and nourish us mentally. Hard as it may be to look after ourselves at such a time, the body is always looking for balance.

Again, this is a very subjective, personal thing. For instance, some of us tend to over-eat when under stress, whereas others tend to the opposite, when stress and anxiety make us feel nauseous and food doesn't interest us. Anxiety tends to weaken the will; as explained earlier, the thinking brain shuts down and we are ruled by our feelings of fear, apprehension, and inadequacy.

**Prompts**

a) Reflect on what you do to de-stress. What are your strategies? How helpful are they? What could you do instead?

b) If you feel caught up in over-coping when under stress, ask yourself how this behaviour started; in other words, how the crisis triggered the habit, how your feeling self takes over.

**NB:** Coping Strategies 2, Section 6.

# Stretching to compensate 1

Childhood relationships and experiences which have dented our self esteem. We feel unloved

Relationships we make in order to make up for losses and pain in our early formative years

## Stretching to compensate 1

## Reaching out when we feel diminished

Looking back to our childhood, if we now feel that we lacked the love we needed; if we have a tendency today to still feel unsure about our ability to manage – relationships, work, money, life! And if we feel undervalued for some reason, lacking in confidence, the chances are that we will try and compensate for what's lacking, to fill the gap and feel better. If things have not gone smoothly at certain periods in our life; our parents' divorce, for example, or significant losses or bereavements; if we have had to look back (up the waterfall) and take responsibility before we were ready; and particularly if we suffered trauma or abuse in childhood, we tend to look for substitutes for the unconditional love we didn't receive. We make relationships with others - people, habits, things - in an attempt to make up for what we have missed.

However, due to our negative experiences, we are more than likely unaware of why many of our relationships either don't last or are at best unsatisfactory.

Such experiences can severely dent our sense of self and, as a result, we push out away from the dent in an attempt to keep the 'ego' volume stable. By this I mean we're trying to find a way of feeling good about ourselves, maintaining a balance as best we can. So we compensate the absence of security by filling the gap with anything that might do instead. This can all too easily not do the job you wanted. Negative residue from the past can be powerful.

**Prompts**

a) Acknowledge any unsatisfactory current relationships, or those you have had, and what it is about them that make or made them so. Try to be honest and clear with yourself.

b) Recognise what's going on and try to identify the causes. Think about the nature and extent of what you'd like to confront and change, and how you might do this.

# Stretching to compensate
# 2

With help, understanding and acceptance we can begin to repair our ego; retreat from the damaging inappropriate relationships; and welcome – or at least come to accept – some of our unhappy childhood memories.

## Stretching to compensate 2

## Re-establishing the balance

All healthy relationships involve a certain amount of compromise; this might feel like, but should not involve, losing part of our identity and true self. Any loss or change is hopefully compensated for by the gains of being in a positive relationship. The whole is more than the sum of its parts.

And yet an unhealthy, destructive or dysfunctional relationship causes damage to our self-esteem as well as to our sense of belonging in the world, our social life – something we all need. In order to withdraw from what is now not working for us in our current relationships – for example with partners, family members, substance abuse, obsessions – we need to be honest enough to reflect on the quality of our life and decide if it is as we think it should be. We might also reflect on what we didn't have in terms of our needs being met through childhood and growing up.

**Prompts**

With help, understanding and acceptance you can begin to repair your ego; retreat from the damaging and inappropriate relationships; and welcome – or at least come to accept – some of your unhappy childhood experiences. Remind yourself of the flow of love, recognising that blame is not part of this task.

a) Write down or record in some way your thoughts and memories of events and relationships which you consider were damaging.

b) What can you do, or are you doing, to find your healthy, balanced self?

# SECTION 4

## UNDERSTANDING OUR RELATIONSHIPS

We are social beings. One of our essential Needs is for social connection, connection with others on all sorts of different levels. So, while we offer closeness and companionship, love and friendship, so also do we need to find safety in loving relationships, confidence in professional ones and above all a sense of self which is strong, authentic and resilient. Being loved, appreciated, respected and approved of is empowering; it helps our confidence and self-esteem which lead to resilience, which we all need.

Part of our make-up is our fundamental need to belong. We all aim for the 'good fit' with our friends, colleagues, family and loved ones. It can be a delicate balance, that of making sure our own needs are met while at the same time considering the needs of others. Sometimes, in our eagerness to belong, we can lose our true selves. When this is happening to us, we're not usually aware; it's only later that we come to our senses. It's therefore important to learn to be self-aware and observe appropriate boundaries between ourselves and others.

This is perhaps work in constant progress and development. It therefore follows that how others see us is also important. We may be misunderstood; we may misconstrue others' behaviour or reactions. Some awareness that our 'normal' is possibly not another's 'normal' will help us navigate our relationships successfully.

# Maintaining boundaries

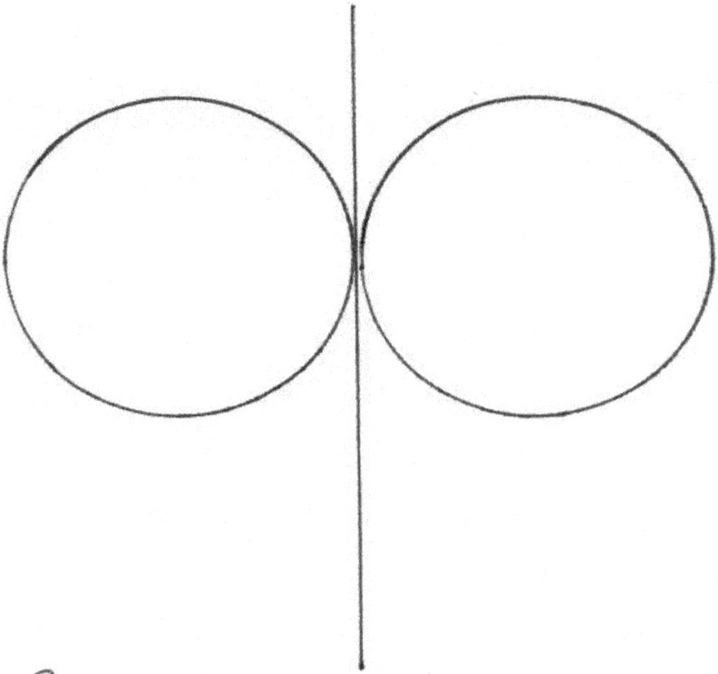

2 separate individuals
with clear understanding
of the boundary between
each other

## Maintaining boundaries 1

One way of seeing how to be in a healthy well-functioning relationship is to consider ourselves as separate individuals with a clear boundary between us; we each retain our own identity, our autonomy, integrity and our self-respect. This way, while living alongside the other person, we don't lose touch with who we are; we don't get bogged down or sucked into the other's stuff or their particular way of being – their 'normal'.

This idea could be stretched to embrace other aspects of our lives, not just with people, such as our relationship with food, exercise, work, housework, politics, in fact our major activities, preoccupations and habits.

For a healthy relationship to thrive it is important that we feel comfortable in it, neither invaded not abandoned but equally together, yet separate, willing to listen to each other with mutual respect for all the differences between us.

**Prompts**

a) In your different relationships how effective are the boundaries between you and the other?

b) How do you manage and enjoy your independence in your various relationships?

# Maintaining boundaries
## Intimacy

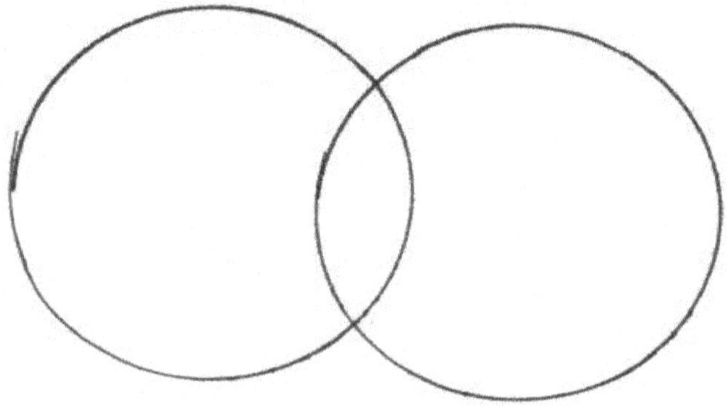

2 individuals choose to share moments of warmth, friendship, intimacy — without losing their sense of self, their individuality

## Maintaining boundaries 2

### Intimacy

Being in a relationship with another is more than merely being together or living together. Such a relationship denotes moments of sharing, intimacy, friendship, companionship, caring; also appreciating and possibly valuing the lows as well as the highs of being together. It does not mean we have to lose our sense of self, our identity or those aspects of our life which are important to us. It is still possible to retain our integrity, our values, our essential self, while linking up closely in whatever appropriate way with the other person in the relationship.

Relationship is about making a choice and a conscious decision to join with another in whatever way that suits the persons involved. Learning when and how to disengage from a relationship, or simply an intimate moment, is equally important; it's about asserting ourselves, trusting our inner strength to be our authentic self in what may be a tricky time. It's about treating others, and being treated by them, with respect and consideration for both their and our needs.

**Prompts**

a) What are your key strengths in the way you manage your relationships?

b) Which aspects of your current relationship do you feel you (both) need to work on?

# <u>Maintaining boundaries</u>

Losing ourselves

Too much dependance
and entanglement with
each other can lead to
losing our sense of self
and so our self confidence

## Maintaining boundaries 3

### Losing ourselves

At its best a healthy relationship is where love, care, trust, mutual acceptance and respect are present. Those in it feel a bond and closeness that transcends everything else around them. Here personal growth can be achieved as each person feels supported and empowered to achieve whatever they're striving for.

This suggests a certain degree of dependence, and, while this could be a positive attribute, if there is too much dependence and over-reliance on each other, it could prove stifling and disabling. We feel trapped, smothered.

At its most negative the relationship could develop into an obsessive inter-dependence in which the individual becomes lost and suffocated in the entangled mix and mess. In a desperate attempt to fit in, self-assertion becomes difficult. We begin to doubt ourselves. Desperate to fit in, be loved, we easily become 'people pleasers'. We're not sure who we are any more. We begin to lose self-confidence; our ego takes a further plunge, and we no longer feel comfortable. We are lost.

In our anxiety we feel incompetent and may therefore easily make mistakes, such as accommodating another's preference, mood, or behaviour, without attending to our own needs or concerns. This can lead to a very unhappy downward spiral in the relationship.

**Prompts**

a) Take care that you don't allow yourself to get wrapped up in another's way of being (their 'normal') which is not yours.

b) Watch out for being overly dependent on someone or something. Face how this feels and ask yourself what you might like to change.

# Giving and receiving

## 1. The need to give

Please accept...

## Giving and Receiving 1

### The need to give

The art of giving and receiving is not as straight forward as it might appear. Giving is a pleasure and a generous way of showing our love, respect and appreciation, according to the circumstances, the relationship and the occasion. While being true to ourselves it is also important to bear in mind the sensitivities and tastes of the receiver. We're not only talking actual objects here, but this also applies to our verbal exchanges. For example, when speaking, we know what we're trying to get across to another, yet we really don't know if the other has received what we said in the way we meant it. This needs to be checked more often than we probably do. Language, tone and speed of delivery, not to mention the expression on our face! all play their part in verbal exchanges. We can be hurt and confused if we're misunderstood.

Giving can also become competitive, as in who can give the biggest, most expensive present…. As this game escalates, things can get uncomfortably out of hand. Children's birthday parties today are a good example of this.

Some people feel an overpowering need to give. This might hide a desire to dominate, to compete, to be loved, liked, popular. We want approval in some way and so wish to please. Or we have a strong sense of obligation to someone. People pleasing might work short-term; however, the receiver is likely to become more and more uneasy and eventually lose respect for the giver. Long-term, so much giving can be exhausting and expensive. We shall not get the love and appreciation we crave with such bribes. And this is not how true friendships are made.

**Prompts**

a) Ask yourself how genuinely generous, is your giving. What drives your wish to give? Is your giving appropriate to the situation?

b) When you speak, do you get a sense that the other has grasped the essential meaning and intention of what you said? If not, what does that say about your delivery? And the relationship?

# Giving and receiving

## 2. Unable to receive

I don't deserve

## Giving and receiving 2

### Unable to receive

Many of us find it difficult to receive; for example, compliments, presents or expressions of affection. We negate, excuse, justify, deny or deflect in order not to show how we feel about the focus on us. We are embarrassed, feel awkward, don't know what to say; if we're not used to being treated kindly and have not learnt how to receive graciously, we won't know how to behave. This can be confusing; it's something to do with feeling self-conscious, not that important, and unworthy of such attention.

Rejecting a compliment or the offer of a present can cause misunderstandings. This can be hurtful to the giver who only means well, and we need to appreciate perhaps what prompted the giving. Not taking a compliment can be a lost opportunity if it's shyness that's driving our refusal. Do we really not want something offered? Or are we too afraid in some way to accept? A classic example of rebuffing a compliment is often heard: Giver says, 'What a lovely jacket!' and we the receiver reply 'This old thing? I've had it for years, it really needs chucking out and...' etc., etc. which to the giver can feel quite dismissive. And thus, we've belittled ourselves as well.

On the other hand, accepting a compliment does a great deal for the self-esteem of both parties.

**Prompts**

a) Notice your reaction to compliments, and how your response affects the giver. When you're offered something you don't want, what do you think about the giver and the giving? What do you do?

b) What might be your reason for resisting a compliment or refusing to accept a gift?

# Thriving in the frame
1.

I am safe and secure
I understand the rules
Boundaries are in place
I know where I am in
this relationship.

## Thriving in the frame 1

This is perhaps a rather rigid metaphor for the structure within which a relationship can flourish. It lends itself particularly to parent and child. It is also the basis of trust, which is so important for our health in all relationships.

We all need boundaries for our security, and, yes, certainly, some flexibility is important. However, there will be limits. If we can understand these limits, and trust that we will be safely held within them, we will both grow emotionally strong and develop a healthy outlook. Such a relationship will work well.

It is our natural drive to push at the boundaries as we grow up, even also in adulthood, wherever and whenever we come up against them. It's a way of learning to face a challenge, daring ourselves to challenge others.

And yet, while we feel compelled to push at the edges barring our way - rules and restrictions which frustrate us - we nevertheless yearn for the reassuring presence of a restraining influence. Deep down we are relieved, we welcome it.

The frame is reliable, trustworthy; against known and unknown, it offers consistence, containment, and predictability. It offers security since it sets the rules within which, and perhaps because of which, we can thrive.

**Prompts**

Make sure to keep any promises you make. Likewise, if the boundary or frame is breached, it's important that you carry out any sanction you pledged. Otherwise, trust is lost.

a) Think about how secure you were as a child. What boundaries come to mind that were helpful or unhelpful?

b) How are your boundaries now?

# Thriving in the frame
## 2.

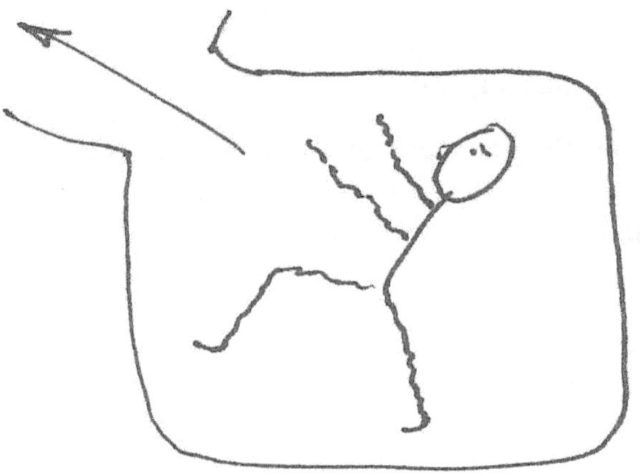

- I am no longer safe
- My boundaries are broken
- I'm feeling wobbly
- I'm unsure what's allowed and what's not allowed.

## Thriving in the frame 2

A good enough relationship is one where the centre holds, and the loving frame is strong; where there is mutual respect, trust, and deep affection and appreciation. When the structure loses its strength and the frame breaks or comes unstuck, the 'picture' is no longer held in place and could fall out and itself break – or fall apart.

If we apply this idea to a relationship, it's not difficult to see what might happen. Some boundary is breached, the edges are fuzzy. We are unsettled, maybe confused, we no longer feel as sure as we did. Both of us might feel this. The relationship suffers: we no longer know quite where we stand and are likely to escape in some way. This might be a way of avoiding each other and/or the truth of what caused the break. Or blame sets in from one or other of us – or both. The resulting lack of trust can feel truly devastating.

We all understand that children need the frame of security, and they learn to respect the boundaries – or not – as they grow up. And if we do not follow through with any promises or threats that we make relating to the by now familiar boundaries, they will act out in some unhelpful way. We will have lost their trust and respect, and our dignity and self-respect. This is bad and confusing for them as it is to us and needs amending.

The need to feel safe and contained is a vital part of our childhood, for this is inevitably carried into our adult relationships. Lack of security and trust in relationships when we're young is all too easily pattern-matched in adulthood.

**Prompts**

a) Recognising fuzzy boundaries in your and others' relationships is a significant start. Understanding their source can be interesting if not intriguing.

b) What might be done to help repair a broken frame and regain the trust?

# Living on the see-saw
## 1

An equal relationship
Both have their feet
on the ground

## Living on the seesaw 1

Our relationships with partners, friends, families, colleagues, even strangers, work best when they are on an equal footing. Mutual respect and a genuine appreciation of each other's strengths and weaknesses are important. Add to these a willingness to listen, and the chances are that the relationship will be sufficiently robust to thrive and develop to deeper levels. Such a relationship means there is trust; we can meet each other on the same level. We retain our dignity and integrity; we feel good, knowing we are heard and appreciated by the other, with sufficient understanding and acceptance - if not necessarily agreement on everything....

Metaphorically speaking, since only we are in control of the part we are playing in any relationship, we need to keep our feet well and truly on the ground and take responsibility for our thoughts and actions. Thus, we are neither dominant nor victim; we each remain 'grounded'. This means being realistic about what to expect from the relationship; and accepting that no relationship is perfect; we have to be constantly assessing and working on it.

**Prompts**

a) Speak your mind, with consideration of the relationship boundaries and the circumstances.

b) As a listener, be respectfully attentive to what the other has to say, even if you disagree.

# Living on the seesaw

2.

| | |
|---|---|
| Top dog | |
| Bully | Victim |
| Aggressor | Bullied |
| Persecutor | Intimidated |

## Living on the seesaw 2

It is a truism that every relationship has its ups and downs, however caring and loving people may feel towards each other. This is because all our encounters are inevitably laden with historical baggage which informs the way we behave and the way we see things. However, for a relationship to work well to the mutual benefit of those involved, there has to be a large element of give and take as well as appreciation of what each has to offer.

When a relationship is characterised by one person wanting to show who is boss, who is in control, needing to play top dog, bully or Mr Right, it is likely that the other member of the partnership will be the underdog or victim. Similarly, if we allow ourselves to be ruled by the habit of not asserting ourselves, we become the victim as this habit has the upper hand.

It may be that we are prone to put ourselves in the 'poor me' category, which enables the other (person or habit) to dominate. Thinking ourselves back to level on the seesaw is the first assertive step – maybe scary, but ultimately confidence-boosting.

Whether we find ourselves in bully or victim mode, this is our perspective, and entirely ours alone; for the way we see things is our own and fed purely by our experiences to date. Yes, our past, long ago or recent. Another example of how our yesterday gets in the way of our today.

To survive being in such a relationship the victim may develop all kinds of strategies. If we expect to be attacked in some way, we have to remain on permanent alert. This is pattern-matching in action; and stressful.

**Prompts**

a) Recognise your own default position. Ask yourself where you are on the seesaw in relation to the other(s) in your life and why you put yourself there. Find a way to ground yourself to prevent either dominating or submitting.

b) What level of control do you have in your various relationships? What could you do to redress the balance?

# Buckets

## 1. Sulking

- If we insist on sticking to our point of view
- When stepping out of our bucket would mean losing face
- We're not even talking to each other? Why so defensive? What do we fear?

## Buckets 1

## Sulking

When two people simply cannot agree, when neither is prepared to listen, when there are strong feelings on both sides and resistance is the name of the game, it seems impossible to break through the barrier we've created.

The emotional arousal in such situations means that our feelings have totally hijacked our thinking – that side of us that is rational and level-headed. Inevitably our capacity to think straight, stand back, understand the other's point of view, assess the situation objectively – all of these openings remain shut. Things feel dreadful, we're poles apart, we're very unhappy, and yet our stubbornness keeps up our resistance; we will not yield. In such a state, while blaming each other, we feel powerless to change the situation.

The idea of each of us stuck in a bucket, unwilling to step out, would draw a smile if it were someone else, not us. The bucket represents the rigidity of our resistance, our determination not to budge from our standpoint, to 'stick to our guns', whatever the consequences.

**Prompts**

a) How often do you find yourself in such a bucket? What put you there?

b) What do you need to do to break the deadlock and step out?

**Ref: Virginia Satir, Peoplemaking**, 1972. Science and Behaviour Books Inc. USA.
ISBN: 0-285-64872-1.

# Buckets

## 2. Stepping out

Assuming those last two questions can help calm us down, we can make tentative moves to step out of our buckets.

## Buckets 2

### Stepping out

When we're emotionally aroused – when our feelings have hijacked our thinking – it's impossible to think clearly and so hard to be objective about how we're behaving.

Somehow our new awareness (from reading this book?) has a chance to kick in with some compassionate logic (is there such a thing?) which will help us to acknowledge our hurt, feeling criticised, blamed, attacked as we do. We can take a deep breath – I know, the first answer to any problem – count to five, then break the silence, saying something to the effect of owning how we're feeling. Remember that, since only **we** are responsible for **our** behaviour and reactions, **we** can influence the way our relationship goes from here. We are **not** responsible for the behaviour or reactions of others and are not in a position to change them. We therefore can only do something about our own. However, this in turn may just influence the other's responses. And dialogue can begin.

**Prompts**

a) When you find yourself in one of these bucket situations, take a risk: Try admitting to your bad or uncomfortable feelings. Use an 'I' statement rather than starting with 'You'. A 'you' statement comes across as blaming which will continue the defensive/offensive stand-off.

b) Ask the other how they are feeling. Really listen to the response without judgment. What happens?

# Relegated to the back seat

- What am I doing here?
- I'm not used to this
- How have I allowed this to happen?
- What does it mean?
- What do I have to do?

## Relegated to the back seat

When we find ourselves pushed aside, made to feel second best when we thought we were at least among the first; when we are deliberately and obviously put down in the presence of others – how do we react? It may have slowly become a pattern, and then suddenly one day it dawns on us how we feel; and we are shocked. We had not realised how normal this behaviour had become and how we had got used to it. Slowly our self-image is deteriorating, and our self-esteem is rock bottom.

If we find our position taken by another, or given to another, on a regular basis, we are likely to feel humiliated and embarrassed. Then more strongly perhaps ashamed, but not sure why. This can lead to despair and misery. We're not sure what to do, speak up or – more likely – present our false self for a while, until we find the courage to face the situation, and the people involved.

We tell ourselves "Clearly I am not good enough". This is most likely the message we were given when much younger; it stayed with us.

**Prompts**

a) If this, is you, be self-respectful and true to your nature: Challenge this undeserving turn of events? At least you will be taking charge of your response to the way you are being treated. Speaking out salvages your self-esteem, whatever the outcome. Remember to use an 'I' statement.

b) Somehow find a way to show your authority and confidence from the 'back seat', thus avoiding the criticism of 'sulking'.

# Needing to possess

If we're very needy
the other person
only wants to run

## Needing to possess

Strangely, like a lot of things, a relationship is much more than the sum of its parts. The number of parts we bring to our relationships is of course countless. The two people involved in a couple bring along to it not only our recently acquired baggage of experiences, but also our historical legacies; these include our childhood memories, conscious and unconscious, of mind and body. Each of us brings our need for warmth, acceptance, care and a sense of belonging. And needs must be met if we are to be a responsible, authentic, healthy and secure giver and receiver in the relationship. Our needs are universal yet unique to us, and their scope/extent is inevitably informed/influenced by our upbringing.

The need to be cared for and looked after can sometimes be so strong that our partner can't deal with us. The relationship is no longer equal if one pulls or pushes much more than the other. Trust, an essential ingredient in all healthy relationships, is damaged; and in our fear of losing the other, our need increases beyond tolerance. The more we need, the more demanding we become. And the more we expect, the more we will be disappointed.

Neediness can be debilitating. We want someone – or something – really badly. Rejection can feel so hurtful and humiliating. If we want someone's love and respect, we need first to let them go. Then they will make their own choice to stay or go. The paradox is that if we feel free to go, we may well want to stay. The hard bit is letting them go in the first place. This takes courage.

**Prompts**

a) What might compel you to not let someone go? Ask yourself what you fear most if your partner, friend, habit, etc. were no longer in your life?

b) Conversely, if you feel overwhelmed by another's need for intimacy, commitment, love you can't reciprocate, how might you deal with that?

# Under the Thumb

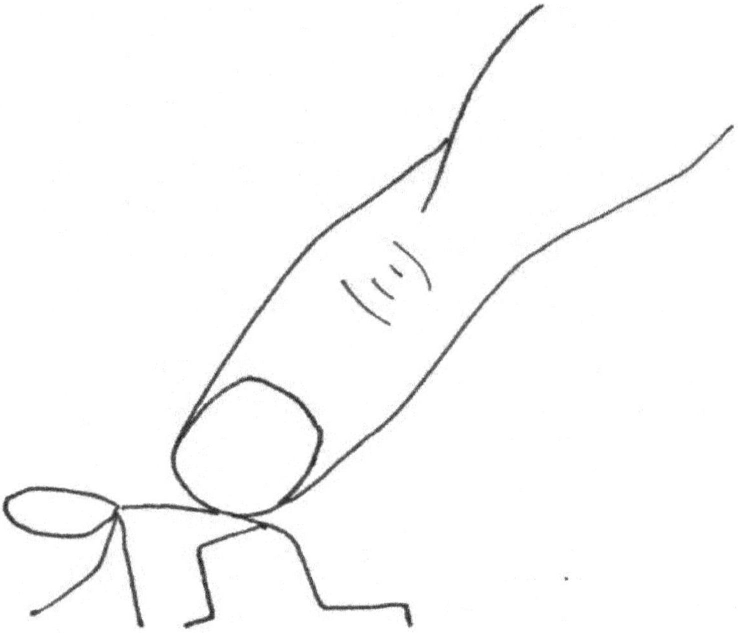

- I feel bullied, controlled
- I keep having to crawl away without being heard.
- I'm tired of being criticised

## Under the thumb

In certain relationships, if we find we're becoming less and less authentic, it's probably a sign that we're not happy and are being nudged or forced into complying with something we're not comfortable with. When we feel observed, monitored, criticised or controlled in almost everything we do, we have no mental or emotional space to be ourselves; stress accumulates until the emotional part of our brain has no room for the logical part to take charge. This is an example of the usual hijacking when we are emotionally aroused; our rational mind seems not to be working, and we become 'stupid'. Whatever we do, it seems it's unacceptable. We feel inadequate and worthless.

We need to find a way of crawling out from under this thumb. Strangely, fear is the driver for both the dominating thumb and our submissive response. If we can remind ourselves that we and we alone are the agent of our choices and actions, then, little by little, we begin to feel we can be in charge. We no longer have to bend to the will of another, and with this understanding we can embark on finding our true selves again.

**Prompts**

a) Whose is this thumb? Imagine what it would feel like to lift it away. What consequences do you fear?

b) Notice if you can when the thumb is exerting its power; prepare to evade it.

# Needing support

## Needing support

One of the most intriguing aspects of the human condition is our need to be seen, heard and respected as a unique individual with the freedom and capacity to do what is best for our wellbeing. Indeed, this need is 'given'. At the same time, we prefer not to be alone all the time; we thrive on and need social connection and support when we need it! These two seemingly contrasting aspects create a tension in us which could drive us on – or hold us back.

This tension seems to me healthy. It is a strength we can use when we are both willing to trust others and also to let go. Seeking support is not always easy; it suggests that not only is there something wrong with us but also that we are unable to deal with it ourselves. And this feels to many like a weakness.

And yet it is no shame to admit that we need support from time to time; especially when we are affected by a crisis. We all know what stress feels like, uniquely to each of us, and we will all have experienced stressful events such as illness in the family, divorce, bereavement, moving house, etc., etc.

At such times, the difficulty arises with our emotional response together with our fear of shame. We may feel too wrapped up in our trouble to ask for support, or even to let others see our pain. Our experiences and our culture or family history will affect how we approach seeking help; it is surprising how many people see asking for help as a weakness.

Yet we like to help, and feel sad and useless when our offer of help is refused.

**Prompts**

a) How easy is it for you to seek support? What holds you back sometimes?

b) How often do you give support? How is it received?

# Social Connection

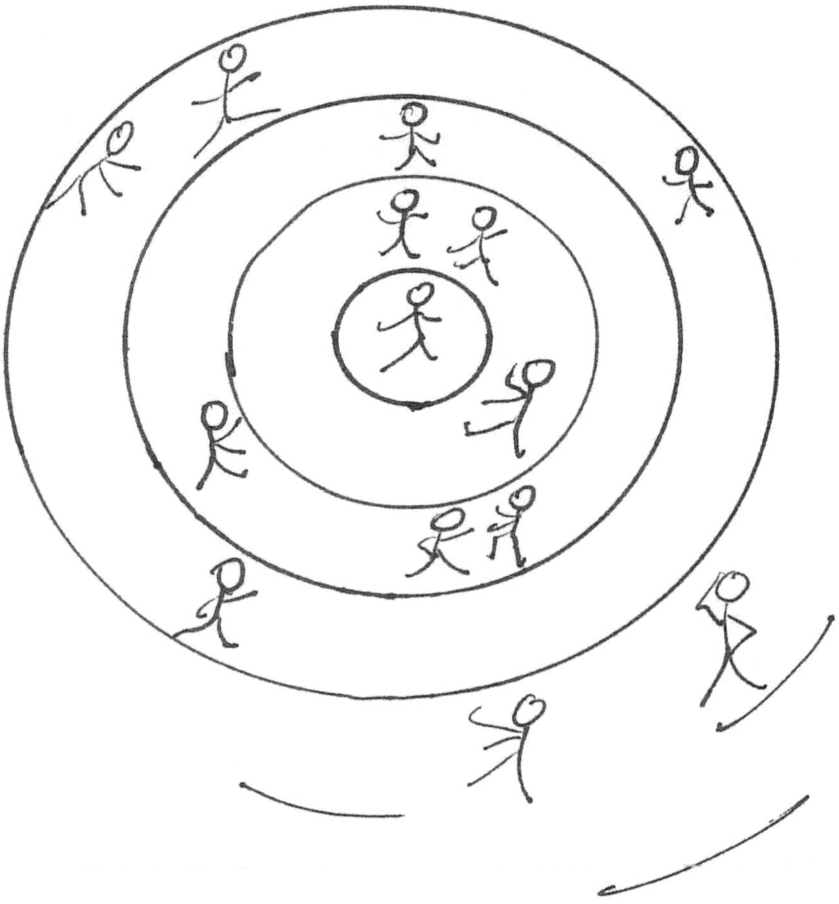

## Social connection

Safety isn't simply the absence of threat but rather the presence of connection. A connection which, in these Covid 19 Lockdown times, has been extremely difficult and in many cases impossible to maintain. All the more reason to find other means, if possible, to stay in touch.

We are undeniably social animals; we thrive in groups, finding status in belonging. Our social connections are vital to a healthy state of mind and so therefore to our well-being. Our friendships flourish on different levels and at different distances, and friends may move in and out of closeness, depending on all sorts of things. Family connections can be strong; they can also be confusing or difficult, often for historical reasons.

With our connecting comes a sense of belonging and safety which are crucial to us as social human beings. Some of us may belong to a family where being 'cut off' seems the pattern down the generations and we're not quite sure where we belong; this is hard to bear; however, we may have learnt this way of being and find ourselves in turn cutting off from others, in an attempt to avoid hurt.

In our relationships, our feelings towards people and activities, relatives and preoccupations can fluctuate according to mood or whim, and of course changing circumstances; however, generally speaking, we have a fairly clear idea of who is close and who is further away in our family/social sphere. And possibly how we'd like to change some of these connection distances.

**Prompts**

a) Draw your own diagram of your social life. Where might you place your friends and acquaintances on these rings? What do you see over all?

b) Where do you belong? What does it feel like? How might you like things to be different? What would you change if you could? And how might you start?

# We are the hub!

## We are the hub 1

We are the centre of all our relationships. If we place them in a constellation of our friends, loved ones and acquaintances, we are naturally at the centre since this is about us, what we see and how we see it. In the same way everyone else has their own constellation and their perception of their social circle, and how comfortable they are at their centre.

When it seems that others are falling out with us, or we with them for some reason; that we're losing friends; or it seems they are drifting away... no longer interested, busy elsewhere... we might ask ourselves what's going on.

We feel rejected, confused, maybe even resentful. Or we may put up a front, pretending we don't care, a good example of our feelings hijacking our thinking.

It seems important to acknowledge the situation and assess our part in it. For, since we are the hub, it must have a lot to do with us. We might wonder what exactly.

**Prompts**

a) Ask yourself honestly what you think might have driven any of your friends away. And were they really your friends?

b) Take responsibility for your part in this and ask yourself how others see you and why.

# We are the hub 2

## We are the hub 2

How different it feels when we are surrounded by true friends with whom we enjoy equal and mutually appreciative relationships. The more authentic we are, the more at ease we feel, and so we're more open to new ideas, creativity, learning new tricks, and a healthy lifestyle.

In this way, if disagreements arise, if one of us is upset and feels free to express it, the friendship will flourish and become richer through being true to ourselves, our nature, and respectful of each other.

We can easily make mistakes in choosing our friends; first impressions are sometimes just that, an impression to impress the naïve newcomer, which may possibly hide the true insecure self, protected behind the mask. Once the mask drops, we may change our minds about the person emerging from behind it. It's difficult being friends with someone who is pretending. And much easier when we can trust each other and share both happy and sad moments with equal understanding and empathy.

**Prompts**

a) What experiences have you had with new friends? How do you know who to trust?

b) What is the test for you of a true friend?

# Connecting

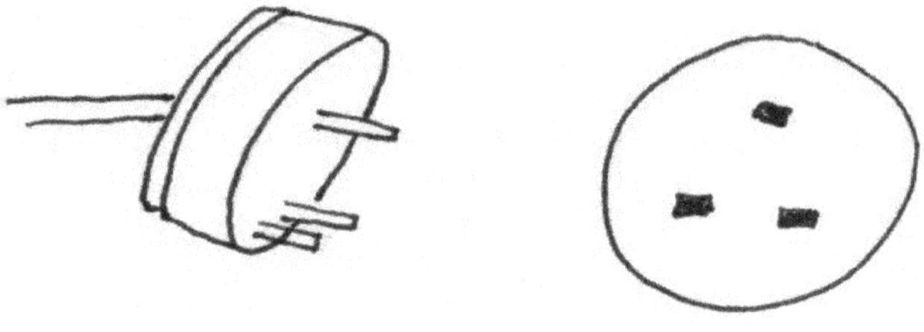

This has potential for connection

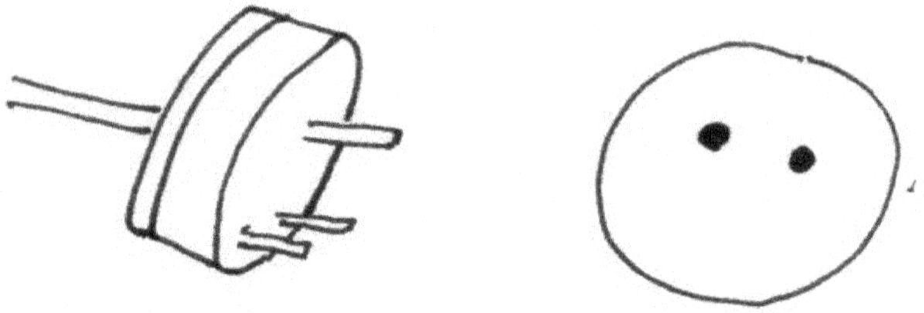

No connection possible here
What to do? Adapt?
Or move on....?

## Connecting

### Socket and plug

Yet another way of looking at a relationship. When there is a comfortable fit the chances are the connection will function well. On the other hand….

We talk about square pegs in round holes, where there is no possibility of achieving a working connection. It's interesting to reflect a little as to how we could make a meaningful connection here. In this case we use an adapter, a middle device which has the capacity to accommodate both 3-pronged plug and 2-pronged socket by linking them to each other.

Disconnect can be a problem in any relationship. When this occurs, we often don't really know what's going on, why the gap between us seems so impossibly large.

There are many ways we demonstrate disconnect, and they're all about how we communicate or not. Verbally, for example: not talking, not asking, not truly listening, not picking up on the other's theme; not explaining, not answering, over-justifying. And physically: we pick up disconnect – disinterest, antagonism, intolerance, judgment, etc. - from voice (both tone and delivery), gestures and posture, lack of eye contact, etc.

**Prompts**

a) If this situation is familiar, how have you been cut off? What do you think it's all about? And how has it been allowed (incidentally by whom?) to escalate?

b) What could and might you do to re-connect? If you think of a means to help, a link to bring the two of you together, what or who would you choose?

# Working as a team

Cog wheels

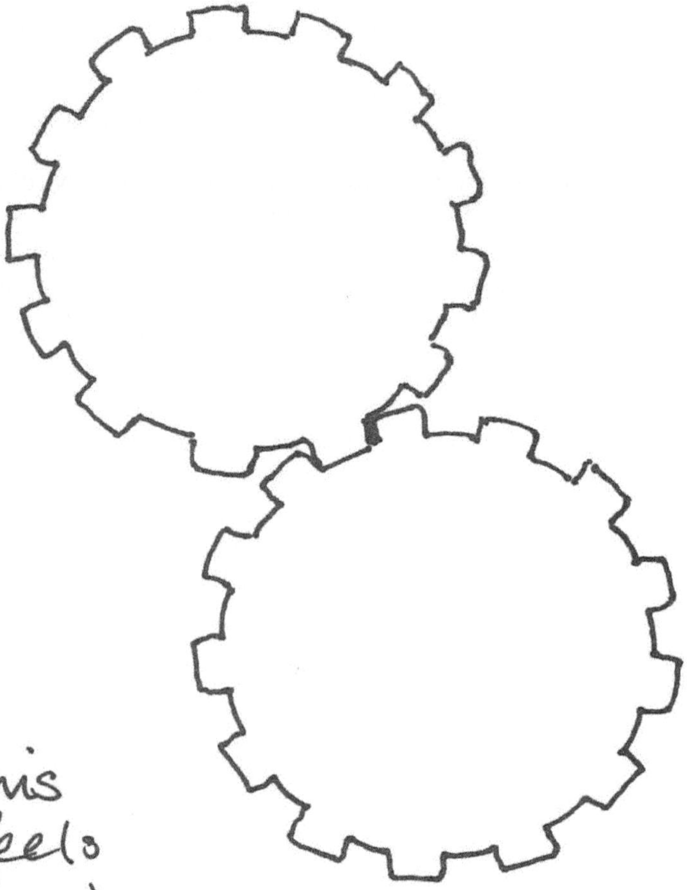

This feels good

## Working as a team

### Cog wheels

Another metaphor. There is little that is more satisfying than when two minds meet, when our opinions and ideas can be openly shared, explored and worked on together. The two cogs maintain their integrity and strength, while engaging with each other as they dovetail.

Whole and complete on their own, when linking with each another the pair becomes much more than the sum of them both. Good feelings and a sense of achievement and satisfaction give us status in our and others' eyes.

**Prompts**

a) Notice when your 'cogs' (mind?) are dovetailing with the 'cogs' of another. Find examples; really feel the pleasure. The benefits of this harmony (another metaphor – yawn?) include increased self-confidence and open-mindedness. How are yours?

b) Notice when the dovetailing does not occur, and how your mood is affected.

## Sympathy and empathy

## Sympathy and empathy

Sympathy and empathy are often confused and, while they are both about emotional expression and connection to others, each has its part to play.

Sympathy is when we feel sad about someone's plight. We express our feelings of compassion and show them in some way that we're thinking of them.

Empathy takes us a step further by making the effort to try and put ourselves in the other person's shoes. If we know someone feels low, 'the pits', we know they need some empathy. If it's you in the pits you need more than an acknowledgment; others' expressions of pity, or tales of their own similar experiences, do not help when we're really down.

It's important to remember that trying to rescue someone from their stressful situation, imposing a solution or advice does not necessarily help. Depending of course on the situation and the needs of the sufferer, 'helping with', as opposed to 'doing it for', is the most effective support we can give.

**Prompts**

a) What kind of support have you recently given someone in distress? How easy was it not to take over?

b) When you last needed support and encouragement, how motivated were you to ask for help?

# Holding bowl

The talker has a lot to say. They can speak freely. The listener helps by not taking personally any angry or emotional outpourings.

## Holding bowl

When we need to off-load, pour out our sorrows and vent our frustrations or confusions, they need a safe place to land. Imagine therefore a metaphorical bowl placed strategically between the agitated, needy talker and the willing, empathic listener. The danger of being either the dumper or the dumped on is avoided, and the outpourings fall into and remain in the bowl where they can slowly disperse in the air.

The listener's responsibility is to pay total attention, neither offering advice nor commenting unhelpfully. Responses such as 'Why don't you...?' or 'If I were you...', etc. do not do the job; they come across as criticism and take away from the talker's need to express themselves. If we focus on the talker's agenda without inserting our own – as in 'I know just what you mean, I had the same ....' - they will feel really heard, which is what they need. I call this last example the 'Oh well, I' syndrome. For an example of a few useful skills, see later Toolbox, Section 6.

If we need to pour out our troubles, we want to be listened to without criticism or judgment, implied or real, and not be interrupted with someone else's problems or experiences.

**Prompts**

The holding bowl can be very freeing and a safe container for both parties, as neither carries away any emotional baggage.

a) If you need to talk about something deeply personal, it is crucial you choose someone who will genuinely listen, not interrupt, or offer advice. Who do you know who might do that? Could you ask?

b) If you have experienced this relationship as either talker or listener, how was it? Note the difference between this way of being together and the much more common way of talking over each other, not really listening and more concerned with what we want to say.

Walking in another's shoes

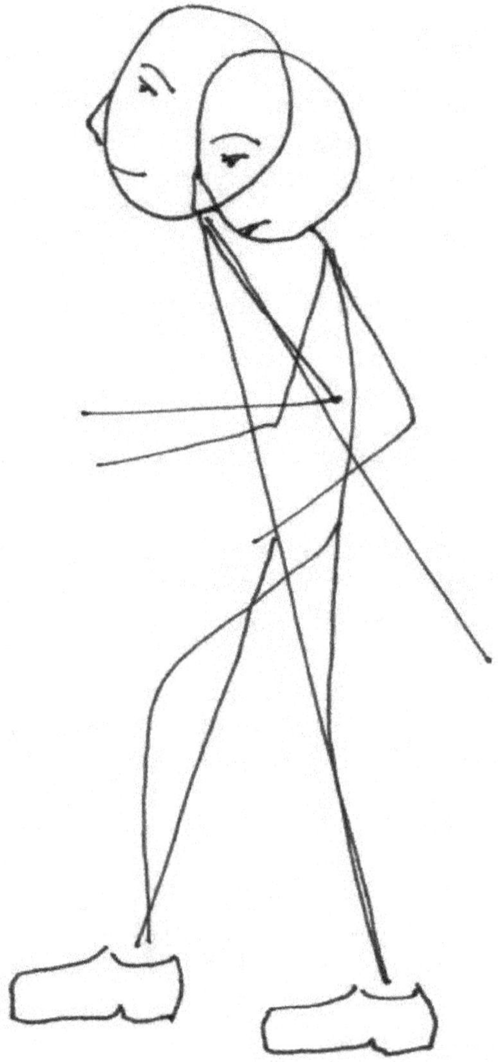

## Walking in another's shoes

This idea is about doing our best to understand how someone is feeling, in order to really try and grasp their situation, and to understand what's driving them to that point. This is empathy, which is different from sympathy. It's not the easiest thing to do because usually we think the way to help someone in trouble is to make suggestions, advise and inadvertently criticise.

On the whole we do not like feeling we are being told what to do, and we get defensive if we feel criticised – at which point, emotional arousal kicks in and we temporarily lose our thinking capacity. So how do we help?

Walking in another's shoes is about being alongside, really paying attention, without judgment, to their plight as they see it, offering support and acceptance of how they're feeling. Being truly heard, they feel understood, validated, and stronger in themselves – more autonomous - and so encouraged to work out for themselves how to deal with their situation.

It's important to maintain our groundedness and not to be sucked into the other person's stuff, while still being in touch with what is preoccupying the other as much as possible.

**Prompts**

a) If this is your role, take care to look after yourself and remember the use of the holding bowl.

b) If you have empathy shown you in this way, you will recognise the difference between this and sympathy; what was the main ingredient that helped you?

# Bus route 1
## The treadmill

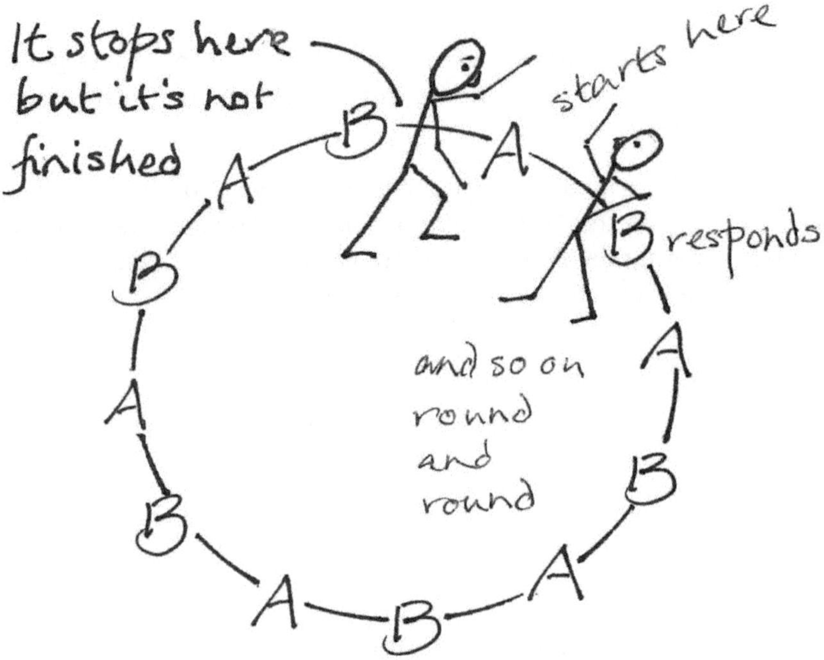


A and B get into an argument over and over again. Same old stuff. Each is emotionally triggered by the same accusations. Feelings drive them rel-entlessly on, rational thinking is lost.

## Bus route 1

## The treadmill

We can find ourselves in a rut at certain points in any relationship. Something pushes our buttons and we're off. We can get locked into a cycle of familiar arguments and conflicts which never seem to get resolved. The physical, emotional and psychological toll on our well-being is immeasurable. It can sap our energy; it can lead to serious depression. When the same issue arises day after day, repeating the same old cycle of frustration and unfinished business, we're in a not-at-all merry-go-round of discontent and despair. We feel perhaps lost in what feels like a heavy inevitability; we wonder with dread where it's all leading. We become re-actors rather than pro-actors; we've lost sight of our power; and we feel out of control.

The idea of the bus route helps us to visualise the journey we're used to being on, and gives us, at last, a chance to choose to get off the 'bus' and take a different route. (see Bus route 2). Our companion will most likely be compelled to follow where we have decided to lead. Now we're our own agent for change; we're on a different route chosen by us, and the journey will take a different course.

**Prompts**

a) What are the triggers that push your buttons? Where does this lead?

b) When you realise that you're on one of your bus routes, what could you now do?

# Bus route 2

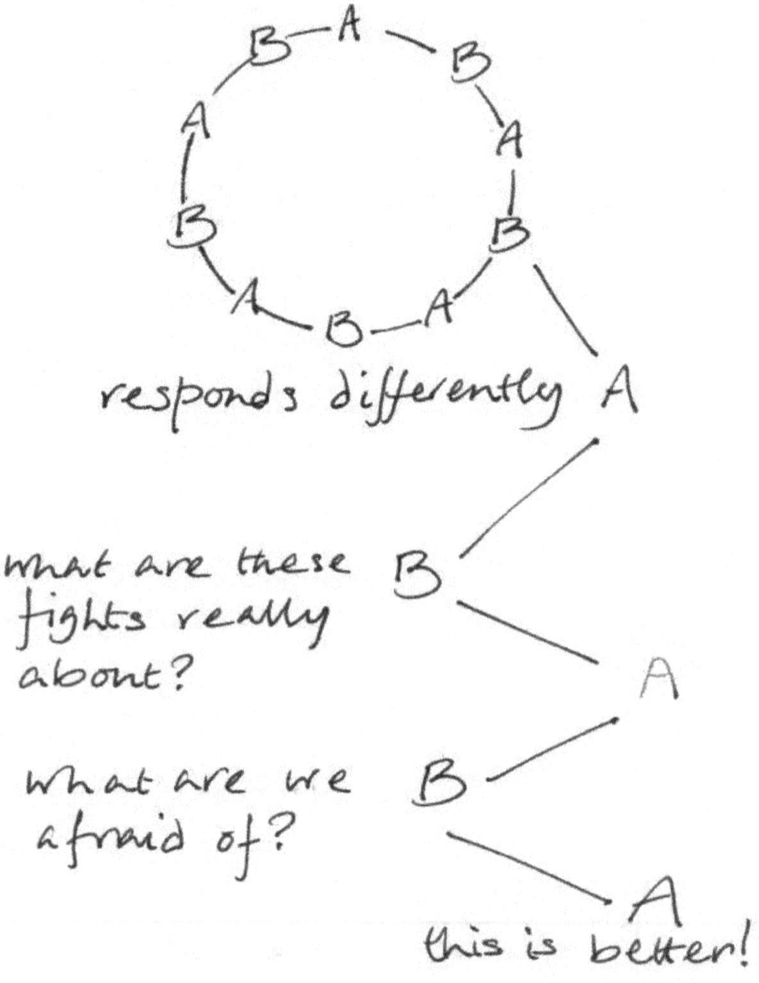
B A B
A A
B B
A B A
responds differently A
what are these fights really about? B
A
what are we afraid of? B
A
this is better!

## Bus route 2

When the same old argument starts up again, and we want things to change, recognising what is happening and making a choice to respond differently from the usual is a start. By changing buses at a certain point on the cycle where it's our turn to speak, we're now on a new route. Our view from here shifts, we have broken the habit (record?) and we can begin to see things differently. Similarly, our companion, who may be taken by surprise, will inevitably respond differently too. How differently we wait to find out. This process might take some time.

We made the break and as a result we feel a little more in charge, rather than being dragged unwillingly along. Thus, the course of the exchange is diverted and altered. A new route for the dialogue is created, and there's a chance now to escape from the old destructive one. To stay with this new experience of relating needs of course constant practice until this way becomes our habit – we could say our new 'normal'.

**Prompts**

a) Acknowledge that both of you are on this bus with the set route, and that one of you can get off and change the whole course of your journey, your discussions. Who knows where that might lead?

b) In what ways would things change for you? For you both? For the relationship?

## SECTION 5

### MIND AND BODY
### THE PSYCHOSOMATIC CONNECTION

This section is about how totally connected are the mind and the body; the 'psycho' in 'phychosomatic' is from Greek, meaning 'mind', the 'soma' also from Greek meaning 'body'. This idea is not as clear-cut as the phrase 'mind over matter'; however, understanding how each part of us is profoundly influenced by the state of the other is worth taking into account. We have all experienced a form of stress at some time or other; and we tend to assume wrongly that it is a purely psychological thing.

The medical model for curing physical ailments tends to ignore the influence of the mind, focusing on the body in isolation. Nevertheless, it happens that a 'somatic' problem can be an indication of mental or emotional stress or distress which is not being acknowledged. Similarly, anxiety can arise as a result of physiological pain. We can see how it gets complicated working out which came first – this is the familiar 'chicken and egg' situation.

The brain's most important job isn't thinking – as we may suppose. No. The brain is responsible for keeping the entire body alive and well. Recent neuroscience findings tell us that, when our brain produces thoughts and feelings, these are more to do with managing the needs of our body than we realise. And this activity of servicing our body is mostly unconscious – beyond our awareness. Briefly and simply, the body's stress apparatus consists of the nerves, the immune system, the hormonal glands, and the brain centres where emotions are perceived and processed. In other words, body and mind are inter-dependant.

'Trauma' comes from the Greek word for 'wound'. The wound leaves scar tissue which is hard and does not grow; and scar tissue has no nerves. I hope you see where I'm going with this. Again, metaphorically speaking, the mask we sometimes wear to protect ourselves from the possibility of being hurt represents our scar tissue, covering up the wound, as in pretending we're fine when we are not. Our public life can be useful in hiding our inner life. And yet, as our mind stays active, it will inform the body if something is wrong, and the body will tell us by reacting with a wide variety of symptoms such as phobias, panic attacks, aches, pains and ailments of all kinds. An example of the unconscious made conscious, as though it needs to be pointed out to us that we are under emotional, mental stress. Well, some of us who are not paying attention may not be aware of being under stress until we reach a point of intense distress.

Neuroscience also tells us that there is no such thing as a purely mental cause of physical symptoms, since the brain is constantly working hard to keep the body in good working order. Anxiety cannot, in itself, be the cause of stomach aches, for example, since both anxiety and stomach aches are each of them different ways the brain has to make sense of the physiological problem. And yet emotional or mental stress is a physiological response to a perceived threat, physical or emotional, whether we're aware of it or not.

During the uncertain and challenging times of the Covid 19 pandemic, our mental and possibly physical lives have been inevitably disrupted, and to different degrees depending on our circumstances. We have all been reminded in no uncertain terms of the importance of physical exercise, enough sleep, the right amount of food and water, relaxation techniques and creative pass times and occupations. The main thing is to do our best to stay healthy, physically, mentally, and emotionally, in order to keep our immune system functioning well and our stress levels down.

**Ref: Your Brain Is Not for Thinking** from **Seven and a half lessons about the brain**. Dr Lise Feldman Barrett, New York Times 23rd November 2020.

**Ref: When the Body Says No; the cost of hidden stress** Gabor Mate. Penguin UK, 2019. IBSN 978-1-785-0422-2-5.

# What is my stomach telling me?

What is this pain about?

## What is my stomach telling me?

Some say: 'the stomach is the second brain'.

When we're anxious we're emotionally aroused and so our thinking brain slows – or shuts – down. Worry inevitably leads to a level of stress, and this releases toxins into our bloodstream. This can very quickly make itself felt physiologically in our abdomen; stomach, bowels, bladder, any one or all of these. This is a normal reaction, showing how intricately connected is the body to the mind. Our body is telling us something important. And the greater the pain, the more we worry. It feels like a vicious circle.

On the other hand, there's something important here about acknowledging our body responses. A bad stomach-ache, for example, that follows a big meal may alert us to visit a medical specialist; however, if the same discomfort occurs in the course of a painful divorce, we might seek out a talking therapist. In each case we experience and interpret the stomach-ache differently.

**Prompts**

a) If you tend to experience stomach pains, see if you can establish the possible emotional connection. Medicating to ease the pain may well help, while dealing with the source of your anxiety is equally important.

b) If or when this happens to you, ask yourself what has most likely brought it on? How can you get the pain to slowly retreat?

**Ref: Your Brain Is Not for Thinking,** from **Seven and a half lessons about the brain**. Dr Lise Feldman Barrett, New York Times, 23rd November 2020.

# Migraine

Aching heads

What is my head telling me?

## Migraine

### Aching heads

Some of us are prone to headaches when we're tired or stressed. Or both. Migraine is a particularly vicious type of headache. I was told as a teenager that my sick headaches were probably a reaction to my school situation. 'School phobia' said the doctor. Looking back now, he was more enlightened than most for the time (1950s). In this case the doctor saw the link between the very debilitating migraines and my emotional reaction to certain aspects of my school life. Needless to say, nothing was done to address the connection between my physical and emotional distress. Today we know better.

The pain of headaches can really interfere with our daily lives and responsibilities. Migraines for example take on a vast variety of pre-, during-, and post-attack malaise, each sufferer experiencing their own unique set of often alarming and dangerously mis-diagnosed symptoms. Again, the physical aspects need some treatment for relief; and the emotional basis or triggers also need to be addressed, since these are possibly the first cause. It should at least be explored.

**Prompts**

a) If this is one of your 'things', how do you manage it?

b) What is the link, do you think, between your physical pain and your emotional / mental state?

# Backache

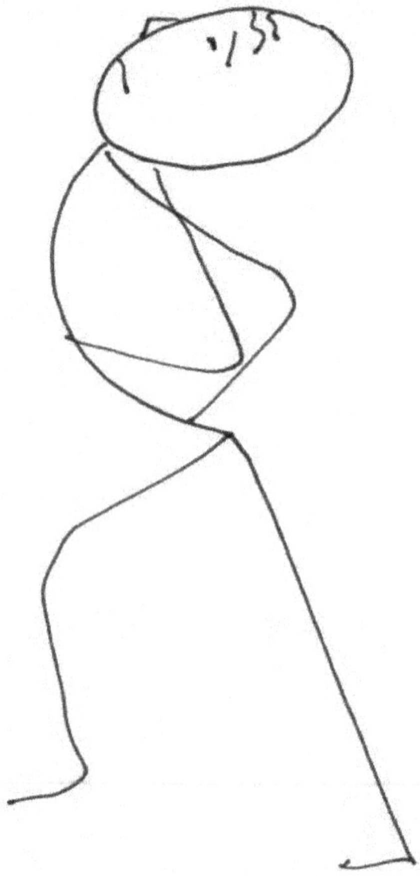

## Backache

We tend to take our body for granted. Until it goes wrong.

Central to our skeleton, our spine is vital to keep us upright. From neck to coccyx – the base of the spine - we rely on the length and strength of our back to support our head and all our limbs.

The back, for many, is an area of the body which is particularly prone to weakness. When we're under stress - worried, exhausted, distressed, depressed… - our back may well be the first victim, giving way most painfully to the point of immobility. Unfortunately, the body / mind connection is not always made immediately. We often don't recognise a strong and socially difficult feeling that's driving us, for instance anxiety, anger, frustration, etc. Again, treating the back pain medically is important; however, ignoring the emotional connection only leaves us vulnerable to similar physical collapse until our stress is addressed.

In my experience, the less likely you are to express your feelings, to be open about what is concerning you or really getting you down, the more likely you are to suffer from backache.

**Prompts**

a) Is this your experience? If backache is one of your 'things', certainly get checked out by a doctor. Ask yourself also what worry, or concern has triggered it.

b) Take good care of your back, and, by being aware of your posture, think about the way you lift heavy things. Or decline such activity until you're sure your back is strong enough. Remember, pain is very often a symptom of stress. What might be worrying you?

# Unusual unexpected signs

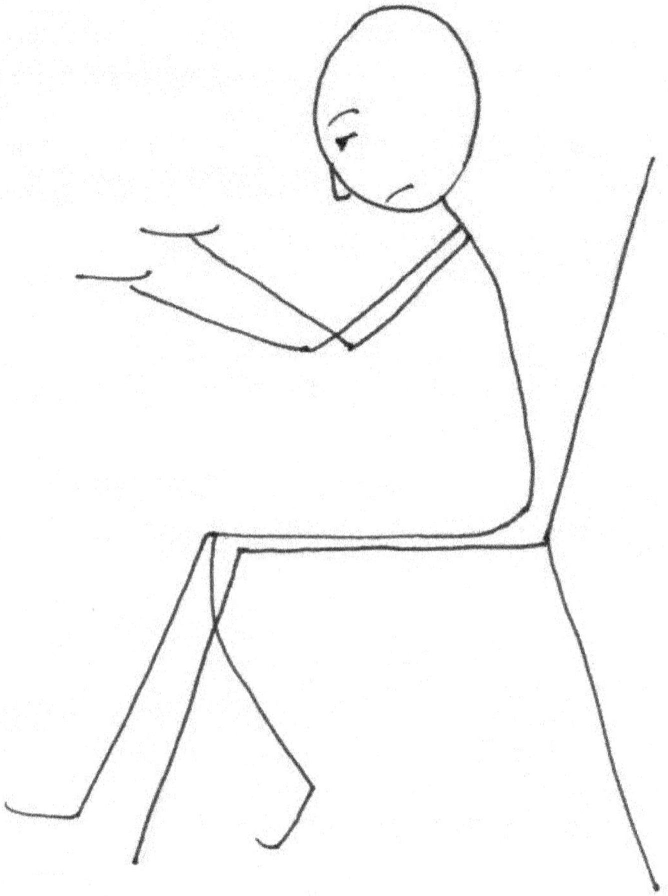

What's wrong with my hands?

## Unusual, unexpected signs

### What's wrong with my hands?

Language can be useful here. If we find a part of our body is behaving strangely, not doing what we ask or expect it to do, we want answers. In this case the hands show signs of eczema, for example, something their owner has never seen on their body before. We know that eczema can appear on our skin as a result to trauma or chronic stress. My response to the above question is 'What do you feel you can't handle at the moment?'

Hands handle things. Simple. Well, let's accept the mind/body connection in that a physical symptom can often be directly related to a mindful or psychological disturbance.

Immediately the symbolism is clear. The owner of the hands knows straight away what seems impossible to deal with, and with that awareness they are able to focus on their current struggle while accepting and understanding the presence of the eczema. They are calmer with this new awareness; and now more able to manage both the emotional and practical difficulties they face as well as the skin disturbance – which in time leaves the hands in peace.

**Prompts**

a) If there is something in your life that you're finding hard to face or manage, where is it physically (somatically) expressed in your body?

b) How might you go about dealing with both the pain and the stress? Which would you address first? Or both together?

I can't walk!!

My legs have given way...

## I can't walk

It is very alarming when we suddenly find we're unable to do the most natural everyday thing – use our legs. There may well be a physiological reason for this, and of course we must check. There also may be, at the heart of this attack, some big emotional issue which is hard to bear. And it's affecting us physically. Why? we ask. Why my legs?

Stress can really get to us and affect us in different ways. How exactly we're affected is a very individual, subjective thing. One thing is sure, there will be a bodily reaction and it will be painful. With the stress we're under – whatever it is about - our mind might be screaming: 'I can't do this anymore!' or 'I can't go on!' or 'I can't stand it!'.

We need our legs to keep us upright to walk and stand our ground.

We are all under a very new and heavy pressure now during the enforced restrictions of the pandemic, both physical and mental, and the over-riding fear that is affecting us on a daily basis, with no certain end in sight. No wonder our own supports give way.

**Prompts**

a) Is there anything you're anxious about which you think is affecting you physically? How does understanding the mind and body link help you to deal with it?

b) Maybe you know someone who has had an experience similar to this suffering person. How might you be helpful in this case?

# Losing our voice 1

Where is my voice?

Am I being heard?

## Losing our voice 1

### Am I being heard?

The voice is a very significant part of us. It has two major functions: the physical and practical noise-making job, and the meaning-making need to communicate, be heard and understood. And then there's the emotional aspect – the joy of singing for ourselves and sharing it with others.

When under stress we're more prone to pick up germs, bugs, viruses. The physiological connections from the brain through the nervous system mean that, when stressed, our immune system is weak and we're more vulnerable to infections.

We can lose our voice when we suffer from a cold and sore throat. We can also lose our voice through stress. The symbolism of becoming voiceless can be found in deep frustration and despair at feeling not heard, not listened to, not being allowed to be one's true self, being bullied and no longer able to cope. All of these and more.

Teachers and singers are particularly susceptible to losing their voice. Both the energetic physicality of constantly using the voice and the confidence and emotional stamina required to 'perform' on a daily basis take their toll.

**Prompts**

a) How has your life – professional or not – involved using your voice? How have you experienced voicelessness?

b) If you can locate the source of your stress, you might also ask if your voice is not being heard, and why...

**Ref: A User's Manual for the Aging Voice** Martha Howe. Compton Publishing Ltd 2020. ISBN 978-1-909-082-61-2.

# Losing our voice 2

I am silenced

## Losing our voice 2

## I am silenced

The voice tells all.

Another aspect of voicelessness begs the question: What are we finding it difficult to express verbally? Our body forces us to be silent. What is silencing us? Who or what is affecting us so badly that we dare not open our mouth? Of course, it may not necessarily be anybody's fault; circumstances are such that we feel under enormous pressure to remain quiet.

Feeling constrained in this way, unable to voice our thoughts, opinions, desires, needs, for fear of negative responses – from punishment through rejection to abandonment – we are left anxious if not frightened.

When we feel something isn't working as it should, and there seems to be an unhappy consequence, we need to recognise the 'chicken and egg' notion - asking which came first. If we're not happy with the sound we make, we feel discouraged; and if we feel discouraged, the chances are our voice will be (heard by ourselves) scratchy. We need to remind ourselves too how easily we can discourage ourselves by what I call 'negative comparison', believing that no-one else has a problem with their voice, only we have.

**Prompts**

a) What is your relationship with your voice?

b) Think about any possibly useful historical baggage affecting your voice and the way you feel about it, speaking and/or singing.

# Emotionally disabled 2

I am in pieces

## Emotionally disabled 2

### I am in pieces

When we feel our heart is breaking and our sadness feels unbearable, whatever the cause, it's hard to find our resilience. It's as though we have no energy, and no emotional room for anyone or anything else.

How we react to grief is a very personal, individual thing. Others may find our way of grieving perplexing. Grief can plunge us into a state where we feel lost, confused and fearful; and often angry.

The physiological effects of our emotional state can take a variety of paths. Anxiety and stress may well take their toll and our mental and physical health will inevitably be affected.

We may feel sick to the point of not eating. We may find getting off to sleep impossible. We may find it difficult contacting people. We will feel very lonely. And when we're tired and malnourished, we don't function well. And here we are again with 'chicken and egg'. Our physical state affects the brain, our thinking is muddled and our emotions in turn affect our body. We are caught in an unhappy cycle. Time and support are what we need here.

**Prompts**

a) Perhaps this expression 'emotionally disabled' does not fit your experience. How would you describe yourself at a very sad and difficult time in your life?

b) What experience have you had of helping and supporting someone through their grief?

**NB:** Emotionally disabled 1 is to be found in Section 2.

## SECTION 6

### RISK AND HOPE

One of the Human Givens ways of explaining some unhelpful behaviours is that we 'pattern match'; from our observation, our learning and the subsequent habits we develop and act out. Of course, if all is well, we don't notice or think about it. It's when 'stuff happens' and gets in the way that we should maybe give some attention to the 'stuff'.

Giving attention to something that bothers or even embarrasses us is not the easiest thing – as you've probably discovered in the course of these pages. Every change we make is a risk, a new experience. Taking that first step can feel very scary; contemplating that first step can keep us gripped, if not paralysed, in doubt and confusion for – well, as long as it takes. Fear of change is often fear of the unknown, fed by our past unhappy experiences of rejection or failure. We expect the same to happen today. For the brain is a pattern-matching organ, relating what is new to what we already know. How often do we not seek the answer to something really important to us in case it's not what we want to hear? Better to have the truth than live in fearful doubt? Hm. How easy is that?

Well, the main thing to remember is that, once we have shifted our thoughts about doing something differently, our brain will gradually adjust. With practice and repetition of both the thought and the action, the brain reorganises itself as it absorbs this new message. The body, which has been storing up its memory, now takes on a new memory, and a new 'normal' for us begins, even if it's the tiniest thing like not saying Yes when we mean No. Such practice takes time, so the other ingredient here is patience – and of course confidence. Thus, having achieved our wish for change, we feel confident, which encourages and motivates us to the extent that we feel competent to have a go at something else. This way we build up a sense of urgency, where we are in charge of our responses to things and people; and, without being bossy or overbearing, we stand up for ourselves when we know it's important.

One very important aspect of our healthy lives, to maintain our morale as well as our physical well-being, is laughter and exercise. Allowing ourselves pleasure and fun along with exercise does us a world of good. During this period of pandemic lockdown, this message is louder than ever. Given the mind/body intrinsic connection, we need to nurture both aspects at once. Playfulness and physical exercise together give the stress hormones a chance to get washed out of our system. Regular physical cleansing in this way will keep us well and stable, fully functioning emotionally, mentally and physically. And this in turn gives us the resilience we need to keep going and enjoy life.

# Learning Cycle 2

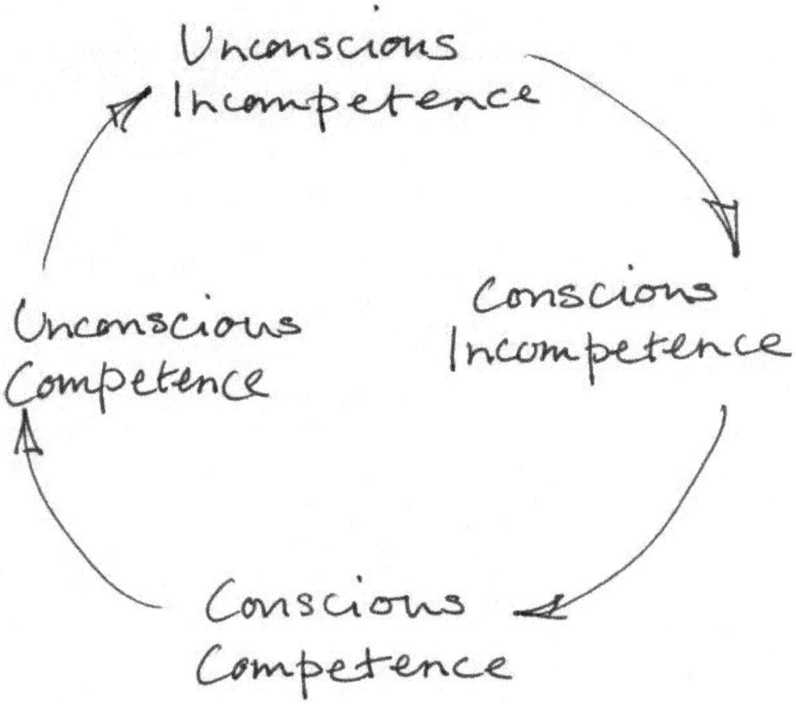

## Learning Cycle 2

### The four stages of learning

Learning new skills can be quite a challenge. We rise to challenge if it's one of our choice and within our grasp – or at least not too far beyond it.

1. Unaware of any need to change or learn anything, we are

   **Unconsciously incompetent**

2. We take something we really want to change or do differently. We set about our plan and make a start. What a struggle it seems. We're not there yet. But it's a common place to be and keeps us energised and motivated. We feel

   **Consciously incompetent**

3. Now we can see some progress, so we're encouraged but realise that, in spite of moments of achievement, there's always more to learn. Most of us would place ourselves at this stage in many of our activities. Seems fine to me. Now, if we concentrate, we are

   **Consciously competent**

4. At this stage we're probably able to 'perform' in many aspects of our lives a lot of the time without having to think too much about it. How easy is this, now we are

   **Unconsciously competent**

**Prompts**

a) Take something you do well and see what stage you're at. How satisfied are you?

b) Perhaps there's something new you want to learn to do. Notice the stages you go through as you progress.

**NB**: Learning cycle 1 in Section 1.

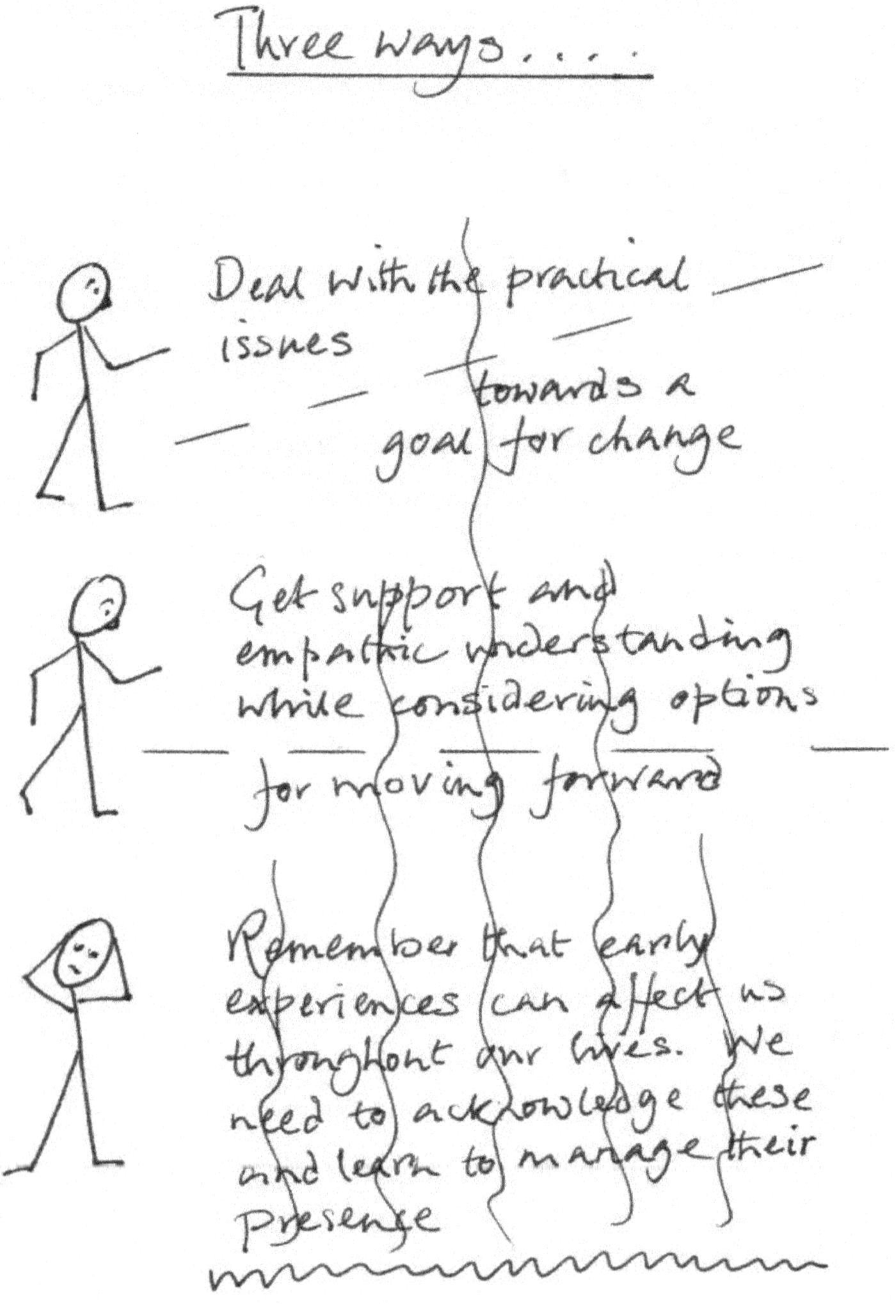
Three ways . . . .
Deal with the practical issues
towards a goal for change
Get support and empathic understanding while considering options
for moving forward
Remember that early experiences can affect us throughout our lives. We need to acknowledge these and learn to manage their presence

## Three ways to look at how to deal with our difficulties

Often when things are not going well, we need some help in addressing what it is that's not working for us. Depending on the issue, here is an over-simplified summary of three distinctly different ways of helping us explore and resolve stuff that's getting in the way of both our well-being and our healthy, balanced relationships.

It may be that an immediate problem has a solution, so go for it (top image). However, we may be in a quandary and need some time to explore our feelings and thoughts before proceeding (central image). Added to these two approaches we must not forget that we are constantly influenced, if not driven, by memories – conscious or unconscious – of our childhood (bottom image).

Given that we are the sum of all our experiences to date (see section 2), and any unmet needs tend to linger unfinished in our psyche, we must be mindful of the blocks that may be getting in the way of our relationships today. Our mind and our body will be harbouring memories of our early experiences; our fears, our relationships, moments, or episodes of happiness, of sorrow, of affection, of hurt, disappointment, injustice, etc., etc.

It may be important for us not to ignore the power of our past while working on our wish to move forward. If something isn't working for us today, we're likely to find the source of it somewhere further back in our life.

**Prompts**

a) What do you find frustrating today? If there is no easy or obvious way forward, where in your life experiences would you start exploring?

b) How risky does this feel for you? How would you go about it? Where, when and with whom would you like to start?

# Growing round our grief

slowly
we grow
around
our grief

we continue
to grow
around it
as it rests
within

## Growing round our grief

Grief and love are inextricably entwined (Grieving 1 and 2, Section 2); if we didn't love so much, we would not be touched by grief. Just as we can't have day without night; or would not appreciate sunshine if we had it all the time. Some may not agree with this last example. However, grief is relative; we are uniquely affected and cannot plan for how deeply our sadness will penetrate our layers of resilience.

The pain of grief can be so strong that we can find it unbearable and try to push it away. In doing so we push others away too. This can result in detaching ourselves from reality; it can take a while to allow other occupations and interests into our consciousness. Gradually, over time, we become more attentive to life around us and we begin to be able to look beyond the blackness of our grief.

While the sense of loss is still with us, it is no longer all-consuming; we build up our emotional and mental strength, and so also physically. In this way our grief becomes smaller in relation to our emotional state. Grief keeps its place in our heart and remains a very significant part of us; however, it is no longer **all** of us, and that's the point. Our grief no longer dominates our life or blocks our progress. It no longer prevents our personal development, our professional life or our relationships.

Balance is restored and enhanced by this extra experience of sadness. With this we are richer, if sadder, people; we are stronger, our capacity for compassion and empathy has blossomed; we have so much more to offer others as well as to ourselves.

**Prompts**

a) If this is something you can relate to, where does your grief reside now? How has your experience influenced your life and relationships since?

b) What other images come to mind? This is so very personal, so how have you grown around your grief?

## Purpose and achievement

## Purpose and achievement

Sometimes we just do stuff, without really thinking much about it. At other times we need a sense of purpose, a reason for doing something; maybe a goal, something to aim for, to keep us on track, in business, connected to friends and family.

Why is this, we ask? Because it's one of the ways that give meaning to our lives. We are aspirers, when all's said and done; we hope for the future, we work towards it with a mixture of eagerness and trepidation, we have plans.

For many of us, thinking **journey** and **arrival** may help us to appreciate the progress and challenges, the struggles and effort – whatever it takes – along the way.

A 'To Do' list represents goals and aspirations. There's a list of chores in section 2. A tick box adds to the journey. With each tick our sense of achievement grows, and with that, surprisingly, further incentive to continue. Or even to move on to the next goal.

**Prompts**

a) What have you achieved in the last week/month? Perhaps not even aware of your purpose or achievement? Now you focus on your achievement, how does it feel?

b) What goals are ahead for you? Thinking about taking your journey in stages, where would you start?

# Indecision

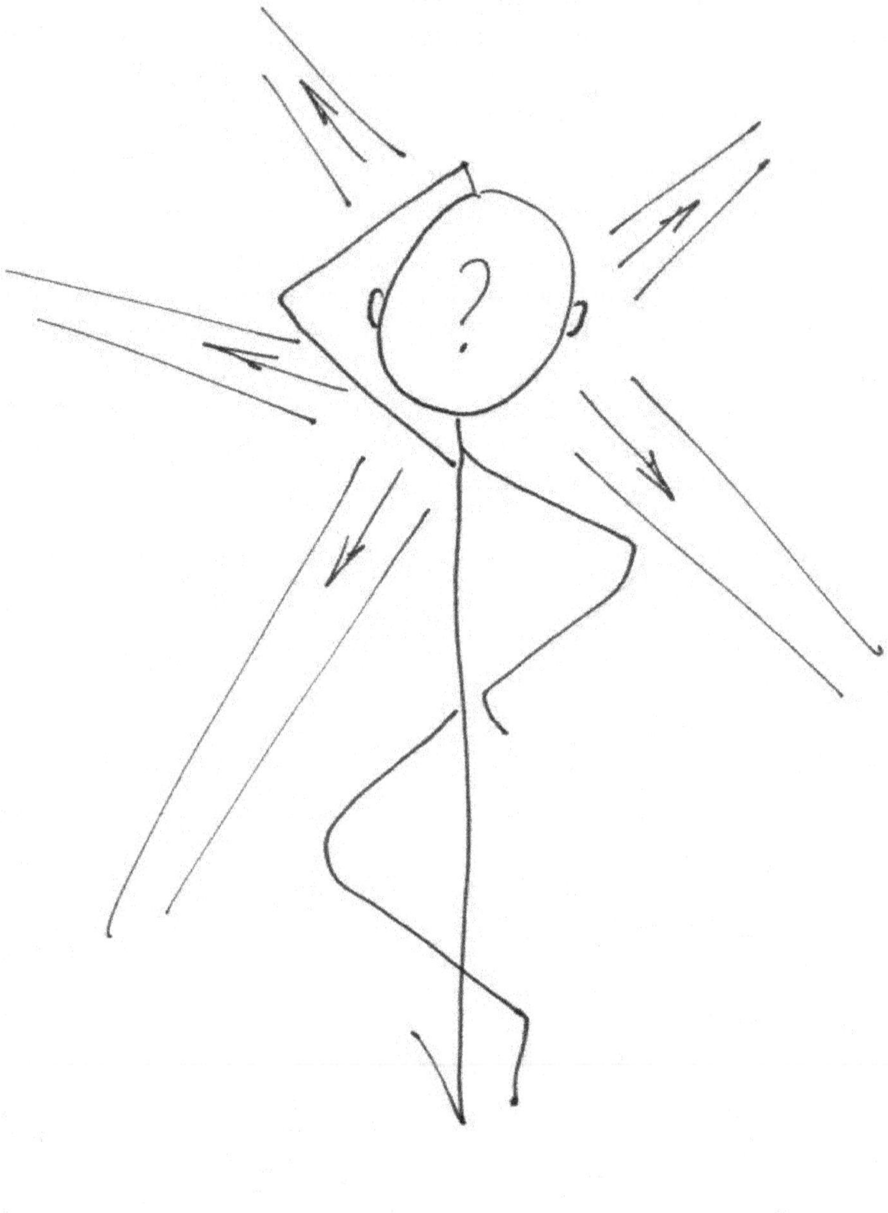

## Indecision

Making choices can be quite a struggle. It's hard to make a decision when we're flustered or anxious. We can get 'bounced' when taken by surprise or pressured to get on with it; and find we've made the wrong choice because we had not enough time to think clearly. A typical example of 'anxiety blocking performance' (section 2).

When faced with having to decide between different possible ways forward, we may feel shaky, uncertain, unconfident, even stuck, the more we worry about it. Limbo land. Purgatory. And, until a decision is finally made, it is a very uncomfortable place to be.

Whatever we do, we do not need or want to be persuaded by another. It's important that we make decisions for ourselves - and own them. Once we have taken responsibility for a decision, we can confidently put it into action. It's then clear who's in charge of our life. We are. That will feel good; and confidence has a chance to return.

**Prompts**

a) How to decide? Weigh up the pros and cons of each possibility? Give each a score out of 10? Close our eyes and place a pin at random?

b) It certainly might help to list the pros and cons. On the other hand, if you can trust them, you could 'listen to your guts'. This last doesn't suit everyone.

# Head above the parapet

How much do I dare?
What's the risk?
What do I want to hear?
What do I most fear?

## Head above the parapet

If we've not been brave enough to look at a situation head on, as we say, it's likely to be because we're scared of what we might see. One way of testing our courage - and resilience – is to take a quick look and see how it feels. Rather like a game of Peekaboo, where the child takes a daring peek to start with, gets braver and braver until they feel free and confident.

**Prompts**

a) How high can you raise your head above the parapet to see what's going on? What about another centimetre or two? What do you have to do?

b) How was that? And who would you like to tell of your achievement?

Stepping stones 1

Moving forward

## Stepping stones 1

### Moving forward

When we recognise a need for change in our life, it can be difficult to know what to do, how to do it and where to begin. The easy bit is to acknowledge the need for change. And, once we have our aim and goal in focus, the more real test is carrying out the necessary in order to bring it about.

Thinking about it honestly, we may soon realise that how we think about ourselves is at the root of how we behave, how we go about things. How we present – speak, dress, choose our friends and partners – all these aspects and more are what make up our way of being and how others perceive us.

It follows therefore that change would require us to start with ourselves, our self-perception, with our limits and potential. For the way we do things is the direct result of our perception of ourselves, whether we're aware of this or not. Others may interpret us in ways we do not intend. The realisation that something is awry between us and them present us with the possibility of change.

Thinking about this with a cool head gives us the opportunity to nudge ourselves into making some changes. How brave is that?

The way to do this is not trying it all at once, but gradually, step by step. Supportive and constructive feedback along the way would be helpful.

**Prompts**

a) Identify and write down what changes you want to make, with step by step, short-term goals.

b) What obstacles might get in the way of your progress? What might hold you back?

# Stepping stones 2

Pausing

## Stepping stones 2

### Pausing

If the stones are too far apart and we're feeling wobbly, the danger of tumbling is strong. This is why we need short-term goals. We may need a helping hand to prevent us from losing balance. We may also need to stand still on one stone while we appreciate the new landing place; here we can reflect on how far we've come and celebrate getting this far.

We can enjoy our new circumstances, enjoy others' reactions or at least notice, and take stock of the difference in our outlook. It's important to take into account that any changes we make can be difficult for others to accept and get used to. Change can be difficult for people. Even our own changes are not without challenge. We need to persevere, and others will get used to the new us – as we will too.

**Prompts**

It's important to remember that we can only change our own behaviour, that changing that of others is not in our gift.

a) What kind of support would be helpful to keep you on target?

b) Whether the changes in your behaviour are short-term or gradually long-term, notice the reactions of others to these changes – if they notice at all! What are the consequences for your relationship(s) of your efforts?

# Stress and Rewards 1

## Stress and rewards 1

The common characteristic of stress is the gradual realisation of our inability to cope with a difficult situation, which in turn leads to feelings of inadequacy or, in the extreme, failure.

Stress is our response to a perception of threat. Such threat will be our own sense of what we fear; irrational as it may seem, if we are frightened, we will experience physical and emotional consequences according to our history, our personality, our circumstances; there are so many different factors to take into account. Its impact can be devastating to our confidence and our ability to get on with everyday life. The feeling of being overwhelmed by commitments, pressures, the demands of others and our sense of inadequacy, can be so all-encompassing, that we lose perspective and find it hard to function well; in other words, get on with our daily lives and feel fulfilled in our relationships. At its worst we might find everything just too difficult to cope with. Disentangling what is truly dreadful from that which is merely irritating or annoying is not always straightforward either.

We experience stress in our own unique way; it is personal and subjective. It is only through empathy that others can fully comprehend and appreciate our experience of it.

**Prompts**

a) Try to identify what is causing you stress. Find a way of itemising the 'stressors' and write them down. What do you see? You may be surprised.

b) Compare all those things you find stressful with what is good in your life. Again, write them down. You may find this revealing.

# Stress and rewards 2

## Stress and rewards 2

We know it is impossible to live a completely stress-free life. In fact, we wouldn't expect to. A certain degree of stress is important for our existence, or we'd never get out of bed. However, it is the nature of the stress as well as its volume and frequency that cause the problems. If stress factors mount up with no sense of reward as counterbalance, then a negative outcome is inevitable, whether emotional or physical, or both.

Yet if the level of stress compared with the level of rewards is equal, this at least can be a comfort. We can continue to function well; we can reassess our evaluation of the circumstances.

If, however, the stress level is higher that the rewards, it is perhaps evident that, in order to relieve some of the stress, some way of readjusting has to be found.

**Prompts**

a) Which stress factors do you have some control of? And which are beyond your control?

b) How do you contribute to the stress levels in your life? What could you change to get, at least, the balance, preferably with more rewards than stress?

# Making healthy choices

## Making healthy choices

Following on from the previous ideas, focusing on self-care and our safety, we do have to make choices which are both relevant to our situation and realistically do-able. Nothing heavy or extreme. A moderate approach is easier to work with.

If we were to mentally and honestly weigh up our healthy and unhealthy behaviours, we would be able to see more clearly how we're managing things. We might be surprised. How aware are we in fact of what we do, when we do it, where and why?

**Prompts**

a) Make two lists of your stress response behaviours, the healthy and the unhealthy. What connections do you make with your past learned experiences?

b) Play around with the different behavioural responses on both lists. What do you notice?

## Noticing the danger and fleeing

## Noticing the danger and fleeing

Some dangers are obvious. With luck, the fight or flight instinct takes over.

Others are less obvious, and it may take us some time to recognise or acknowledge the danger. We may sense it somehow, feel it in our guts, yet be unable to identify or even name it. In our unknowing and confusion, because things don't feel right, or quite safe, we may allow or tolerate its presence – hoping it will go away?

How can we help ourselves if it's not obvious? If we don't trust our instincts? In this state of inaction, we will have symptoms of anxiety – any one or more of the following, depending on our psychosomatic tendency: rapid heartbeat, sweaty palms, shortness of breath, sudden or persistent headache, sinking feelings in stomach or bowels, to name but some.

If we can acknowledge the relevant symptoms, and take care of ourselves, we can make the link between our anxiety and our very real pain, possibly a somatic reaction, telling us that there's a problem. The first thing to do is to focus on breathing steadily, gather our wits, as they say, and doing our best to absent ourselves from the situation, both mentally and physically.

**Prompts**

a) How do you react emotionally and physically to danger? Where does your anxiety settle in your body?

b) What strategies would you or could you put in place to try to move from danger to safety?

# Escaping into safety

What am I fleeing?
Where am I going?
Why?

## Escaping to safety

When we don't feel safe it can be hard to know what to do. We need to run but may not have a clue where to, or how. This is a fight or flight situation. And we are too afraid to fight. With the fear, confused feelings of shame and guilt, alongside resentment and bitterness, are tumbling around in our head. Our fear is so great that the emotional arousal will most likely hijack our thinking brain. This, it can be imagined, does not always help in such a situation. Instinct has taken over.

The fear of repercussions, unpleasant consequences and the inevitable self-blame can keep us inactive for years. Fleeing to save ourselves and our loved ones is one of the most difficult things anyone has to do. And for many understandable reasons we tend to wait too long before taking this brave step.

There is often a long time-lapse – years? – between knowing we need to escape and having the courage to do it. We keep hoping, or fooling ourselves, that things will settle, and it will be alright. However, during that period we need to find a way of reminding ourselves that we're OK, we're stronger than we feel, we are worth more, we have lots of friends, and that we have a right to choose. We need to remind ourselves that we have resources we can use.

**Prompts**

a) Think up and repeat as often as you can a couple of simple affirming phrases that do the trick for you, to boost your ego, recover your self-esteem and keep you going. A week or so of this and notice the gradual change in your outlook.

b) Don't hide your fears. Share them with appropriate friends who will support you in whatever you may need. This may include professional help.

# Assertiveness

In aiming to be assertive, the passive person may feel they're being aggressive - out of their comfort zone - and others may perceive this too. We need to persevere. With time we, and others, will soon get used to it.

## Assertiveness

We often mistake assertiveness for aggression; perhaps because when one person sounds sure of their position or opinion, others feel a bit threatened – a not uncommon sign of insecurity regarding their own position or opinion. It is important to remember that we are each responsible for our, not others', response to a situation.

On the spectrum from aggression to passivity; from bullying to compliant; from controlling to suggestibility, assertiveness straddles the centre. It is a positive, authentic, responsible way of being. It's healthy and satisfying to assert ourselves, saying clearly and confidently what suits and what doesn't suit us. We are not dismissive or judgmental, but respectful of others' views while not losing sight of our own. We may sometimes sense we're shifting towards one end of the spectrum or the other, so - once again, it's good to be aware.

Assertiveness means using our ability to communicate with clarity, thought, consideration and confidence. It discourages aggressive, judgmental or bullying behaviour in others, so avoiding the self-doubt wobble factor in us.

This is a learnt and practised response. While some of us can seem to manage quite well, others need time to learn how to stand up for themselves in an effective and non-destructive way.

**Prompts**

a) Where are you on the spectrum? Think of certain people in your life and note your level of assertiveness with them.

b) How easy do you find dealing with difficult or rather aggressive people?

# Protecting ourselves 1

shield

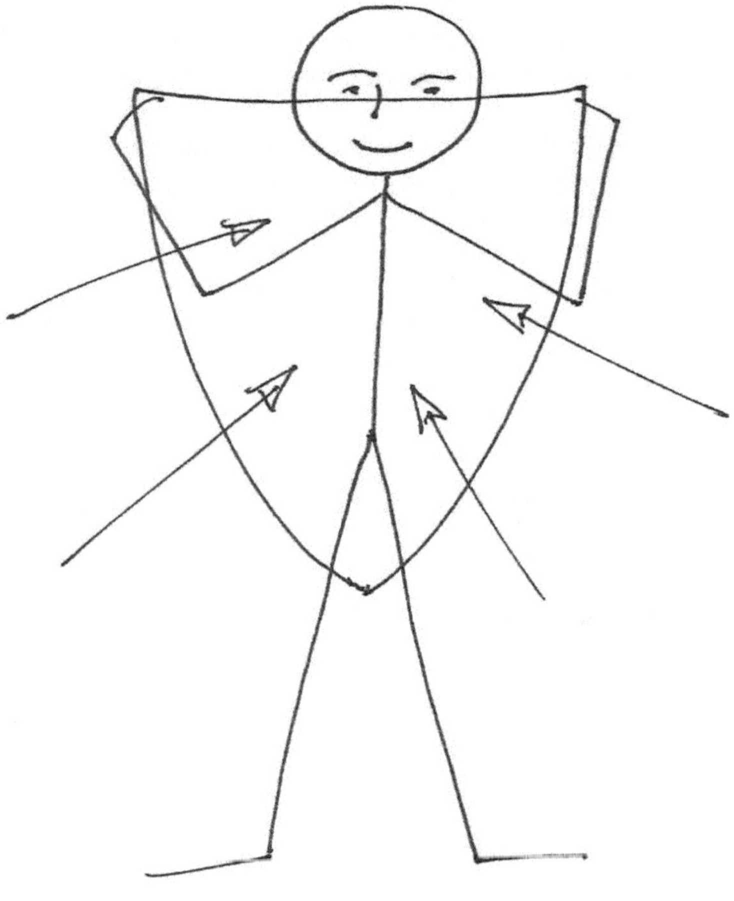

## Protecting ourselves 1

## Our shield

When we're feeling under attack, inferior, or in low mood, how do we look after ourselves? It may have become a habit to feel victimised. The more we find ourselves in victim mode, the more we perpetuate this state of mind. The shield is a metaphor for avoiding being hurt by the 'arrows' of criticism or insults that are coming our way. If we think we'll be hurt, the chances are we will be. If we can **think** the shield, we're at least half-way to being unaffected.

**Prompts**

a) When have you last felt victim to this kind of attack? Go to that memory and imagine your shield taking the hits, leaving you unscathed.

b) Try this with other instances where you've felt put down; get used to a new way of responding. How does this feel?

Protecting ourselves 2
untouched by verbal attacks

## Protecting ourselves 2

### Untouched by verbal attacks

Alternatively, or after practising with the shield idea, we can work at imagining letting the arrows of verbal attack whizz past our ear, not connecting with the body at all. We see them; acknowledge them; and let them fly past.

Although they say, 'Sticks and stones will break my bones, but words will never hurt me', this is not inherently true. Many of us are liable to be hurt by harsh words, and all of us to a different, very individual degree. Remember that we receive messages according to our own agenda; to a large extent this means that we hear what we expect to hear, in other words what we already think or know.

If we are the attacker, there is no real knowing how our words will land, or that their intended meaning will be grasped. If we wish to be kind, the verbal delivery must reflect kindness and bear in mind the state of the receiver – as best we can.

None of this is easy; it may require a lot of thought, which of course is often omitted in the moment. We all need to be more aware perhaps of the possible sensitivities of others.

**Prompts**

a) With actual arrows (very dangerous) you would have to move your body to avoid impact. With verbal arrows all you need to do is **think** 'avoid', so that you are emotionally unaffected. This takes some practice.

b) You may notice in others whether they are practising self-protection in this way. Observe and take note.

# Resilience 1

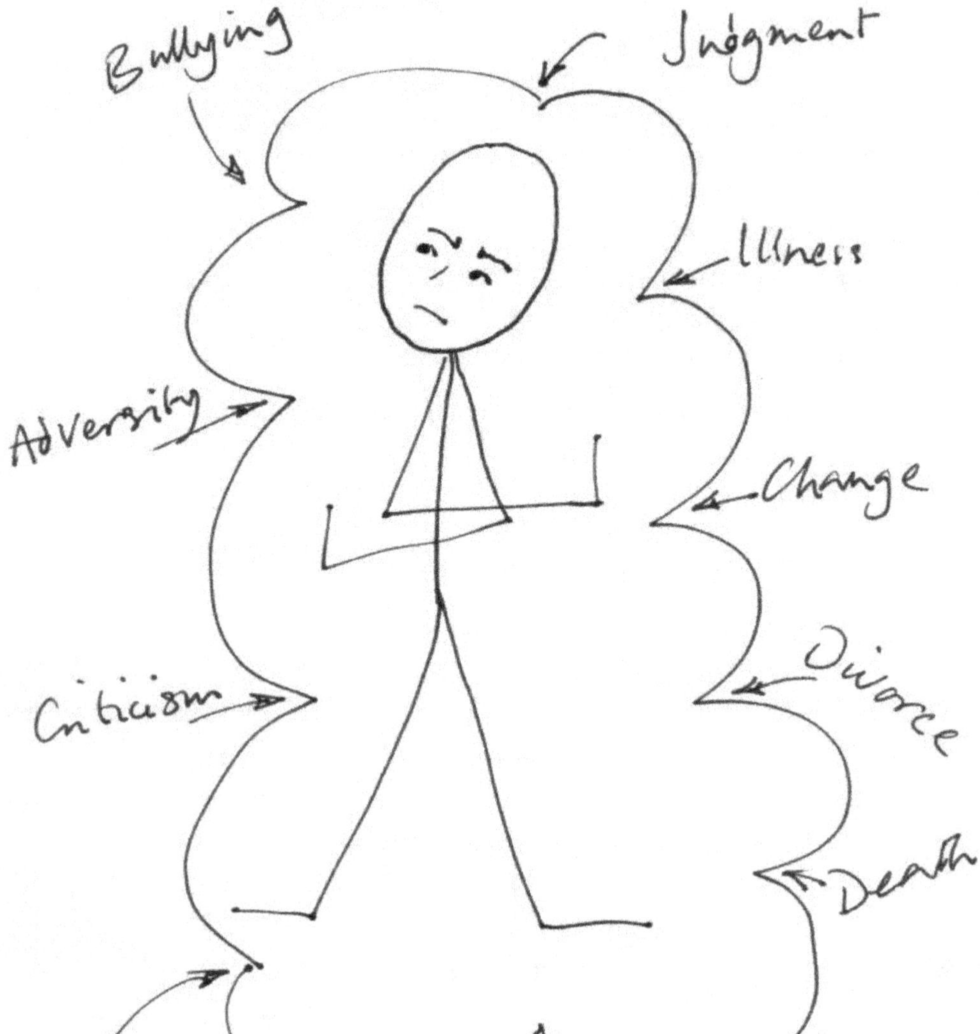

## Resilience 1

Resilience is the process of coping well with stuff that comes our way to challenge us, and the capacity for this is in our brain – our innate resource.

When faced with adversity, when tragedy overtakes us, when losses and disappointments hit us; when we feel threatened, when hard decisions must be made – we need to remind ourselves of our core human strengths, our resources, which help us to meet our needs and keep us healthy. Courage, social connectedness, an instinctive drive to explore possibilities and a creative mind open to change and opportunity can all play their part here.

Instead of falling into despair and bowing to what feels like the inevitable, we could see the situation as a chance to take a different view. This is particularly hard when multiple circumstances are stacked up against us – as for example today, 2020 and most likely beyond, we plough through the Covid 19 epidemic.

If we can take a deep breath and step aside to look at our situation dispassionately, we may glimpse a slither of light through a crack in the door. One door closes, another one opens, so they say. Gulp. In every case? We have to believe it. Our drive to survive means we will call on our given resources to find the strength to face whatever has to be dealt with.

In this way we can be transformed by our capacity to cope and by having managed. Our learning experience and sense of achievement make us richer and wiser.

**Prompts**

a) Recall an episode where you crumpled in a difficult situation. Think what you might have done instead, what resources you might have called upon. Imagine you showed resilience. How does that feel?

b) In what way have you shown resilience recently? Who noticed? What was the result?

# Resilience 2

## Resilience 2

How do we find the strength to carry on when we feel under constant threat, when our very nature, our whole personality, seems to be under attack? It's difficult to defend ourselves without returning the attack.

How to take the assertive position when we feel pushed to the ground on the metaphorical seesaw? A little help and support from a good listener will help us find our inner strength which has had such a thorough battering. For there is no way to counteract a bully except by asserting ourselves and turning our back to them. The bully will not change until they have an epiphany moment; our reaction, our behaviour, is for our benefit, as our job is to rescue ourselves since we can do nothing about the other.

We therefore have to build our resilience and learn how to live with it. Our intrinsic nature will not change; however, our flexibility of mind will help us shift our view of the situation and get on with our lives. Seeming to be impervious to the bully's undermining behaviour is the best way to snub them and save ourselves.

**Prompts**

a) If you have suffered from harassment or bullying, how did it affect you? What were the consequences?

b) How might you help someone who bullies? Would you want to?

Skating on thin ice

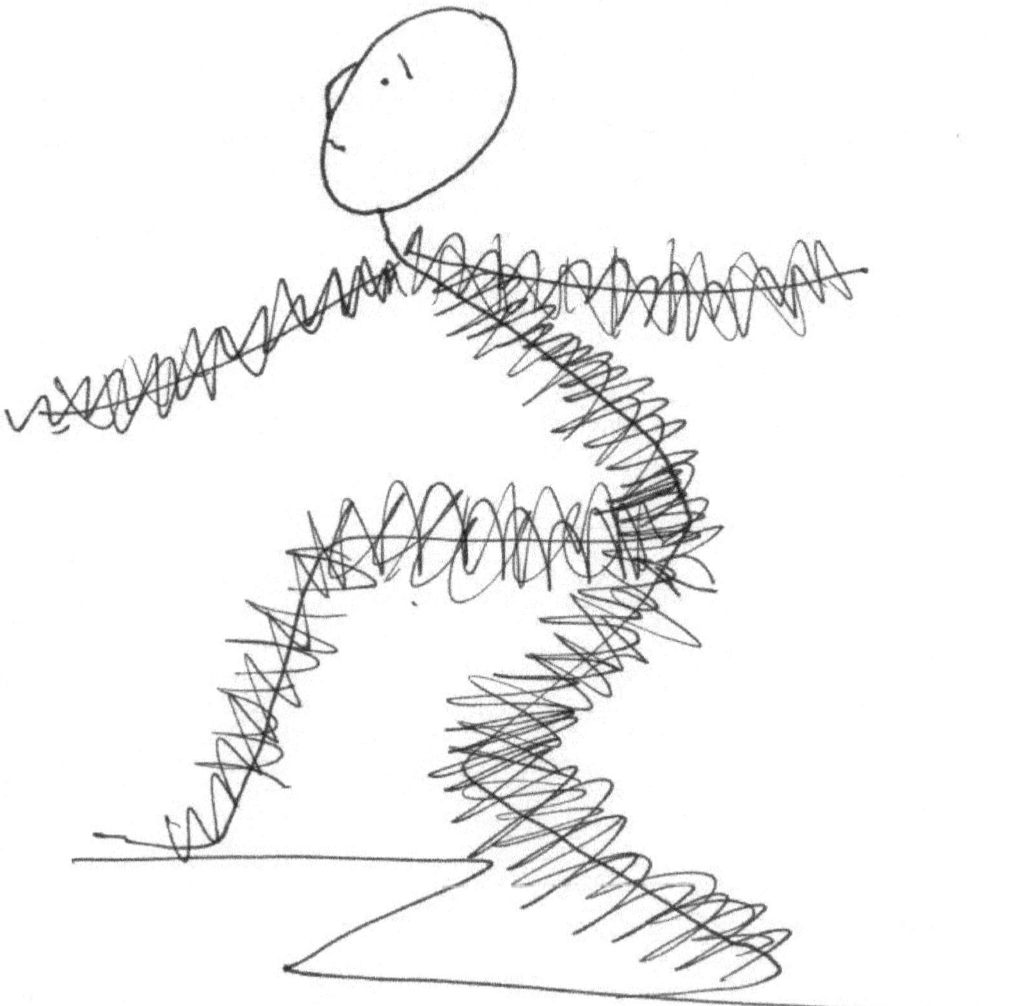

## Skating on thin ice

Sometimes we find ourselves in situations where we feel we simply must speak out; but the moment is such that we fear offending. Or it's a familiar environment where we know we have to hold our opinions in. This is not comfortable, and not good for our simple explanation of authenticity. If this happens often, we could get used to it, and not saying the important thing that's on our mind, or not doing what we'd prefer to do, becomes part of who we are. It might well be to do with needing to fit in and getting sucked into other people's way of being. Wanting to accommodate in order to keep the peace, we lose our assertiveness and begin to feel down on the seesaw. Not good.

Rocking the boat, sticking our neck out, upsetting the applecart – all these phrases represent the sense of danger involved in speaking out. This is something most of us have experienced. We're worried about how what we say will be received, whether it will have repercussions for us and our relationship with the company we're currently keeping. It depends also on our need to belong; this is crucial to our social human nature; it's vital if we want to be approved of, liked and respected.

Is it a risk worth taking? Is the metaphorical ice thick enough to take the weight of our assertiveness?

**Prompts**

a) If this situation resonates with you, how have you handled yourself? What happened? Did the sky fall in? Another phrase we use.

b) If you feel you haven't managed to say your piece when you really wanted to chip in, next time this happens - take a risk.

# Coping strategies 2

## Coping strategies 2

We looked at coping strategies earlier in section 3; how, when we're feeling really vulnerable, in shock, needing reassurance and comfort, we turn to habits which in the moment meet our needs but which in fact could do us harm. Here let's look at different ways of looking after ourselves in times of stress, healthier ways which contribute to maintaining body and soul in a healthy state sufficient to keeping us fit to surmount and survive.

We can easily forget our basic needs; we take our body for granted and may not even think consciously about our mind or our emotional life. When we're feeling down – stressed, depressed, let down, betrayed, whatever – we tend to lack energy; motivation and initiative seem to desert us, and we take the lazy way out.

Some of our needs that need to be met to maintain our holistic health are pictured here. Of course, there are lots of things we can do which give us pleasure and soothe our soul; it's a question of personal choice, taste, and decision to do it.

**Prompts**

a) When things get tough and you need a pick-me-up, how easy is it for you to choose a healthy coping strategy? What would you rather choose?

b) What would your lists of each set of strategies look like? Healthy or unhealthy, to which you tend to reach?

**NB:** Coping strategies 1 in section 3.

Taking charge of ourselves

## Taking charge of ourselves

Taking charge is about managing ourselves, being authentic and autonomous, in our relationships, in whatever situation we find ourselves. And yes, it can feel risky.

A few things for us to remember when it looks as if the relationship feels flaky:

- being assertive
- being self-aware
- using our confidence and competence with new understanding
- thinking our preferred position on the seesaw
- bearing in mind the state of mind of the other person
- being careful to show that we are listening and will not judge.

Sounds difficult? Remember we are not expecting perfection and are always in a state of striving towards it.

**Prompt**

Now include additions of your own to this list. You will enjoy the challenge and the sense of achievement.

# Getting the best out of people

**Encourage**

Mm...
Tell me more

**Nudge**

Yes, I can see...

**Motivate**

Sounds good

**Advise** You might, could, should, ought...

**Command**

That's an order!

**Bully**

Get on with it! Or I'll...

## Getting the best out of people

We all need encouragement, we like approval, and mostly we want harmony rather than discord.

If we want an 'equal' relationship it's important to find some middle ground; whether we're asking a child to carry out a task, an adult to help out with something, or anything where a discussion might ensue. The best method is to find a way of encouraging the dialogue.

Years ago, research into the self-esteem of nursery children concluded that, for every negative 'stroke', four positives were needed for the children's self-esteem to stay healthy. Jennifer Broadley writes about her 5:1 rule – to engage and maintain a useful level dialogue, we must be mindful "to give at least five complimentary, positive or kind comments for any one criticism or feedback".

If we think we're helping another make a decision, we don't start from the bullying end of the spectrum; we stay with encouraging, and, if appropriate, we continue to encourage, nudging them on to a point where they're open-minded enough (due to the gentle way they've been treated by us!) to make their decision. Telling them what to do, or doing it for them, even hurrying them to make a decision before they're ready – well, that does not work.

This way we remain respectful of the other's position and a trusting, dignified dialogue is achieved.

**Prompts**

a) How patient can you be when you want something done? What encouragers would you use?

b) If you can find an example of when you didn't manage the nudging, what happened?

**Ref: Jennifer Broadley**, Couples Casebook **Human Givens** Vol 27, no. 2, 2020.

# Feedback Sandwich

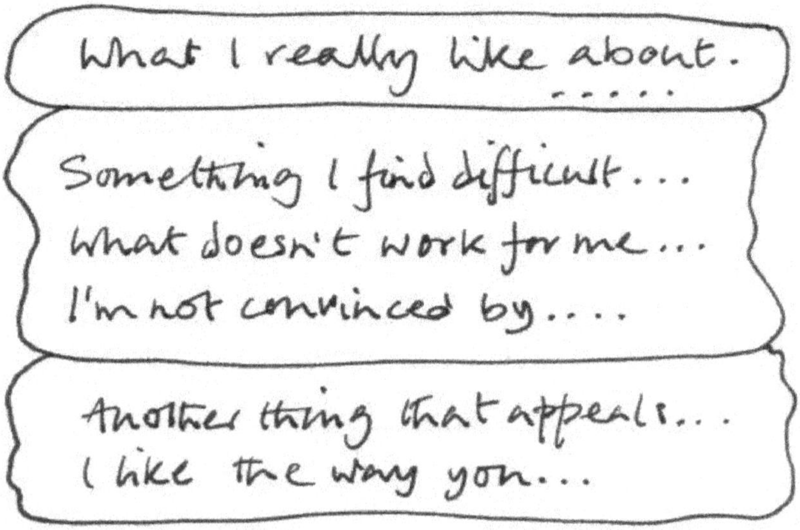

## Feedback Sandwich

Another way of encouraging and motivating another, in whatever it is that they need, is the feedback sandwich. The point of any feedback is to help another to see how their behaviour, or performance – or any aspect of them – comes across to us. Bearing in mind that our responses are our own, no-one else's, they are none the less valuable. The feedback sandwich idea brings together many of the ideas, metaphors, and analogies of this book.

It is important to know how others see us, since we usually want others' approval, if not their praise. We are not helped by negative judgment. Evaluation is hardly ever straightforward, so there is always something positive to say.

If it's about something we've made – a cake, a painting, a Lego tractor, even this book for example – it is genuine, authentic, honest critique that we want, not platitudes such as 'That's nice' or 'I don't like it'. Even, as I once heard, 'That's wrong!' about a piece of art. Generalisations have little effect. We want our more objective critic to be specific and notice the detail; this way we have the chance to hear what has gone well and what needs working on. And the less positive sandwich filling is softened by the positive outer layers which contain the important and encouraging element. Thus, we are not diminished by what feels like the negative filling. We are encouraged to carry on; our confidence is enhanced which means we also feel more confident. We need reminding that confidence and competence influence and inform each other.

**Prompts**

a) What kind of critic are you? Perhaps the sandwich idea helps you to say if and how you don't like or approve of something. Give yourself a feedback sandwich. How easy is it?

b) Ask someone to use the sandwich idea to critique something you've made or done. How does that feel?

# Using the skills box

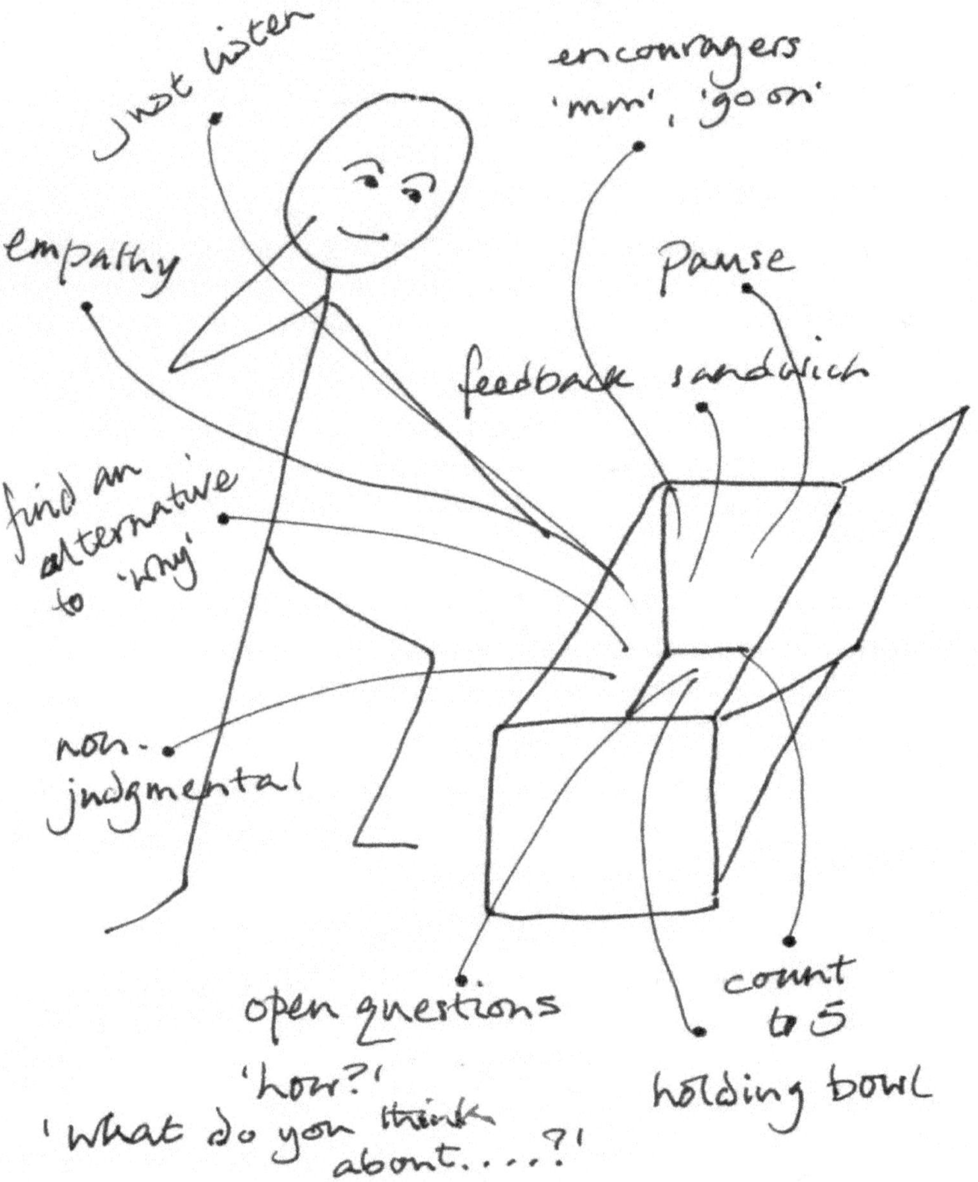

## Using the skills toolbox

As we come to the end of this collection of reflections on human behaviour, and responses to events and each other, I offer here a very brief summary of the sorts of things to bear in mind when we want to communicate well with others.

When we want to achieve or maintain a level and equal relationship, where we feel strong in ourselves and 'in charge' of the moment, the most important element is our relaxed and positive presence. Add to this the toolbox; this represents some of the resources we now have, both familiar and new, to use when and how, as appropriate; to manage ourselves in our relationships, and to maintain them at a mutually and appropriately respectful level.

They are all designed to encourage us to listen to others, to open up, be true to ourselves and help others to do and be the same; to be respectful and accepting of our own and others' emotional state; to recognise when things aren't working; and work together on putting them right. We don't always succeed straight away; with new-found confidence and a sense of competence, we can look ahead, knowing there's a chance. As with most things, it's a question of constantly working at it.

**Prompts**

a) Imagine your toolbox. What is it like? What was already in there? Add more tools that you think ought to be there.

b) Which of these skills have you used recently? How effective were they?

# Playing

## Playing

The main things about learning something new are enthusiasm and patience. A new skill can take time to get good at; see the stages in the learning cycle further back in this section. Our agility and dexterity will undoubtedly improve with practice.

Let's say, week after week we apply ourselves to regular badminton sessions with friends. We may well be all over the place to start with. Hand/body/eye coordination will become more fluid, and any embarrassment regarding our performance will gradually vanish. We'll learn to tolerate all the shots we miss, the people we crash into and the (silly) mistakes we make. We have fun, we laugh a lot. Laughter is another ingredient to our well-being.

And we know how important it is to keep fit. Physical exercise improves physical and mental functioning. We work our lungs and muscles to keep fit and we feel good and pleased with ourselves for the achievement.

Such activity fits so many aspects of keeping ourselves healthy; physically, mentally, emotionally. And among other things, a classic example of Purpose and Achievement.

**Prompts**

a) What have you recently taken up? How are you doing with it?

b) If this doesn't work for you, thinking of your well-being, what would you choose?

## Serenity prayer

Grant me the Serenity to accept the things
I cannot change

The Courage to change the things
I can

And the Wisdom to know the difference

**Reinhold Niebuhr 1892 – 1971**

## IDEAS FOR FURTHER READING

If you're interested in exploring some of these further, and pursuing themes which have resonated with you……

……here is a selection of very accessible books and journal articles which have underpinned my thinking and my work over the years, and which you may find useful.


AXLINE, V (1964) **Dibs: in search of self**
Pelican, London. More recent editions available.

DE BOARD, R (1988) **Counselling for Toads, a psychological adventure**
Routledge, London. ISBN: 0-415-174-29-5.

CASEMENT, P (1985) **On Learning from the Patient**
Routledge, London.

CASEMENT, P (1990) **Further Learning from the Patient**
Routledge, London.

GRIFFIN J, TYRRELL I
(2013) **Human Givens: A New Approach to Emotional Health and Clear Thinking**
HG Publishing. ISBN: 978-1-899398-31-7.

LERNER, H (1997) **The Dance of Intimacy**
Harper and Row, New York. ISBN: 0-06-016067-7.

LERNER, H (2014) **The Dance of Anger**
Harper and Row, New York. ISBN: 0-04-44866-8.

LERNER, H (1997) **The Dance of Deception**
Harper and Row, New York. ISBN: 0-04-440931-1.

LERNER, H (2004) **The Dance of Fear**
Harper Collins. ISBN: 978-0-060881-58-4.

MATE, G (2019) **When the Body Says No – the cost of hidden stress**
Penguin. ISBN: 978-1-785042-22-5.

PETERS, S (2012) **The chimp Paradox – The mind management programme for confidence, success, and happiness**
Vermilion. ISBN: 978-0-091935-58-0.

SANDERS, P (1994) **First Steps in Counselling**
PCCS, Ross-on-Wye> ISBN: 978-1-898059-14-4.

SATIR, V (1972) **People-making**
Science and Behaviours Books Inc. USA.
ISBN: 0-285-64872-1.

SMITH, MJ (1975) **When I say No I feel Guilty**
Bantam, New York. ISBN: 0-553-13715-8.

THOMAS, N (2000) **When Love in not Enough**
The New therapist: working with Human givens
Vol 7, No 3, 2000, p16.

TYRRELL, I (2017) **The Wonder of Uncertainty**
Human Givens. Vol 24, No 2, 2017, p38.

VAN DER KOLK, B
(2015) **The Body Keeps the Score – Mind Brain and Body in the Transformation of Trauma**
Penguin. ISBN: 978-0-141978-61-1.

WINN, D (2011) **Human Givens: in our own words**
Human Givens. Vol 25, No 2, 2018, p38.

WINN, D (2018) **Why Emotions are Sensational**
Human Givens. Vol 25, No 2, 2018, p38.